T0195795

BUILDING A BEAUTIFUL, BETTER LIFE

STATEMENTS TO KICKOFF YOUR DAY FOR A BETTER DAY

REVA BOGGS

WESTBOW
PRESS®
A DIVISION OF THOMAS NELSON
& ZONDERVAN

WestBow Press books may be ordered through booksellers or by contacting:

WestBow Press
A Division of Thomas Nelson & Zondervan
1663 Liberty Drive
Bloomington, IN 47403
www.westbowpress.com
844-714-3454

ISBN: 978-1-6642-9918-4 (sc)
ISBN: 978-1-6642-9919-1 (hc)
ISBN: 978-1-6642-9917-7 (e)

Library of Congress Control Number: 2023914089

Print information available on the last page.

WestBow Press rev. date: 09/26/2023

TABLE OF CONTENTS

ABOUT THE AUTHOR

Before retiring, Reva was a productive, esteemed customer service representative and employee with MCI Telecommunication (MCI - now part of Verizon). She took initiative in providing premier service to her customers and continued to go the extra mile.

She created an effective product for her customers which MCI upper management fully embraced. They rolled out her creative idea to all of its major, national, and global customers' nationwide. Each of these divisions was a recipient of her concept.

MCI valued the details which the tool brought to their clients. Shortly afterwards, she became a respected participatory customer service manager.

Reva retired seven years after relocating to North Carolina from California. After she retired, she traveled around the country in an RV. She enjoyed the scenery throughout the fifty states and the lower provinces of Canada and Nova Scotia. Her favorite places were the national parks and RVing in Alaska.

Reva studied transformational success principles and was certified as a dream builder coach and life mastery consultant. Reva guided people in making their dreams come true.

Reva continues to encourage people to improve their lives and values as followers of Jesus while living according to God's commands for a more joyful and peaceful life.

She enjoys seeing people live their soul's purpose which brings harmony to their lives.

Reva believes the first step toward a richer, more fulfilling life is the starting *gate of change.*

INTRODUCTION

This book is a tool to assist you in understanding the benefits of living a better life each and every day. Allow these sayings to encourage you and direct your thinking, your words, your actions, your habits, and your life. Who and what we are is very important to the world around us and as individuals and to one another.

Daily open your heart to new ways of creating a more peaceful, loving, and satisfying mental attitude and life. Allow new thoughts to guide you away from the worries and concerns of the day.

Allow these statements to stir within you a desire to keep *free* from bad, ugly, and negative thinking that is draining you of your energy and keeping your mind entangled. Meditate on a couple of these fragments each day to improve your day.

You can start anywhere you wish in the book—even in the middle of a page. You may jump around, allowing the book to fall open wherever it may, or just open the book wherever you wish at the time you want to read. Treat this book as if it has no beginning or ending. You will notice I have rephrased numerous thoughts throughout this book. Repetition is the key to remembering.

Use your gift and share the goodness you have within you by being encouraging and supportive to all people. My desire is to equip you with reminders of how to live and be a servant of God, our King. He is the Ruler over all things.

If you are *not* currently reading the Bible, let this book be a starting point to shed some light on the Scriptures for you. If you are reading the Bible, let the statements be quick reminders to increase your self-esteem and your faith as you listen to these truths.

Let these statements inspire you to build a firmer foundation, and to experience a more secure and peaceful life. Our mission is to love one another as Christ loves us, and to stay centered on the way Jesus, the teacher, taught.

We exist to serve our Lord and to live as one church with many bodies (1 Corinthians 12:12), to strengthen an ever-growing community of faith, and to love others as we love ourselves (Matthew 22:39).

ACKNOWLEDGMENT

It goes without saying that a project such as this is never completed in a vacuum.

First, this book is dedicated to my grandchildren: Sarah Boggs, Deacon Bletchley-Boggs, and Dakotah Tanczuk, who were my inspiration for the book.

Second, I want to thank God for nudging me to have it published. Now, my prayer is that this book will get into the hands of people who either don't read the Bible or have little or no biblical knowledge or who need to be encouraged to live a better life. May they experience a desire to read God's Word - The Bible - often.

From beginning to end, I have had the support of WestBow Press-Publishers who were instrumental in allowing me to see the culmination of a dream I had. WestBow Press was extremely helpful in numerous ways, and I am very thankful to them for their professionalism.

I also want to thank WestBow Press-Publishers for providing video materials and lectures from experienced authors regarding their process of writing, marketing, and publishing a book. These materials were extremely helpful with many great tips. Thanks to the authors who shared their knowledge with those of us who have dreamed of becoming an author.

I want to thank Denny Irion, a neighbor, who also gave his time to proofread my manuscript.

I want to thank a life-long friend who read my manuscript and helped me by making suggestions which were invaluable. Thank you, Esther Schrage, for encouraging me along the way with your support.

RELATIONSHIPS

Just as salt makes a difference in the flavor of food, we need to make a difference in the flavor of the world around us, in a good way.

The most tragic thing is a broken relationship with God. The second is a broken relationship with your spouse and children, and the third is a broken relationship with your father and mother.

Before marrying decide against divorce from the start and build your marriage on mutual commitment. Support each other's interests and talk every day, sharing yourself and your thoughts. Come to an agreement before taking any action. Always communicate about everything – all subjects.

Daily communication needs to be a high priority—a top priority in your marriage. No subjects are off limits. That's right, *nothing* is off limits (except gifts for birthdays, gifts for anniversaries, and surprise gifts for your spouse).
(Contact me through my website if you want a *Communication Tool* to assist you in talking about all subjects with success.)

In your marriage and in all your other relationships, truth, and trust should be high priorities as well as your daily communication.

"Walk in wisdom toward them that are without, ... Let your speech be always with grace, seasoned with salt, that ye may know how ye ought to answer every man" (Colossians 4:5-6 NIV).

Put God in the center of your life and marriage; allow Him to rule in your life and marriage.

Don't let the obstacles of relational differences cause you to get in the way of your happiness and joy.

If you fail in keeping your promise, ask the person to forgive you: in person, through a written letter, or by calling him or her.

Accept each other's imperfections and help others to see their wrongs in a gentle way.

Always accept your mate and others for who they are, allowing them to be their authentic selves if it's not damaging to you or others, and continuously be forgiving to one another.

Two honesty, compatible people can have a happy and healthy marriage.

Expecting perfection in each other is unrealistic. Be a builder, not a destroyer, of relationships.

When you think of others' faults, whatever they are, *see* if the same applies to you. Often our own faults are the very faults we first see in others.

Jesus said, "Every kingdom divided against itself will be ruined, and every city or household divided against itself will not stand" (Matthew 12:25 NIV).

We need to be encouraging, loving, supportive, and uplifting to others, while guarding our thoughts, hearts, minds, and reactions. This is the way you and I need to be in all situations and relationships.

Be willing to help others in their suffering, even when it is inconvenient for you.

Honor what you agree on with others. Let it be the right action and the thing to do.

God can reweave the fabric of our lives - healing and mending us, and our relationships.

Repair your relationship with God if it is shattered, and your relationships with others if they are shattered.

Be the exception in unhealthy relationships and stay obedient to God as His servant. Always hold yourself accountable to God and His laws so you do not have to go it alone.

Relationships or activities that lead to sin need to stop.

Stay alert. Close relationships with sinful people will defile us. It's so easy to sin.

To be faithful to your mate, or friend, while you are physically in that person's presence, yet not be faithful in your mind, is breaking the trust that is so vital for a strong healthy relationship. It weakens the intimacy and connection within your precious relationship.

God prepared us in advance to do good for others. We need to encourage others, help others, show kindness to others, befriend others, and uplift others. We are God's hands and feet.

Make a point to do one good deed every day.

Put things aside for the sake of God and people. Honor people and God.

Someone said, "Believe that everyone likes you unless they tell you otherwise."

"If a man say, I love God, and hateth his brother, he is a liar: for he that loveth not his brother whom he hath seen, how can he love God whom he hath not seen" (1 John 4:20 KJV). Our attitudes toward others reflect our relationship with God.

Our desires need to be focused on doing good as well as being loving and forgiving to those who wrong us.

Allow God to revive your life by reading His Word and building a relationship with Him.

"But he that is greatest among you shall be your servant" (Matthew 23:11 KJV).

Don't remain self-absorbed or self-obsessed. Share your abilities and gifts with others.

Caring for others is what brings us smiles, and what brings us together for greatness. When we focus on others, our world expands as problems drift to the outer edges of our minds and seem smaller.

Joy comes in reaching out to others only when it's for the other party. It's the right thing to do.

Understand that how we treat the poor and other people reflects our true character. Never look down on anybody.

Anyone who does not help God's people—the poor, the oppressed, the elders, the widows—is God's enemy.

Help those who are needy. Give generously to others from your heart. It's not what you have in your purse or pockets; it's what you have in your heart.

Many times, all that is needed from you is a listening ear and an understanding heart for a person to feel some comfort.

Forgiving others has a liberating effect on us. The effect is far more for our own well-being than it is for the ones we forgive.

OUR THOUGHTS

Feed your mind with more nutritional thoughts and enjoy a much better life by thinking thoughts of pure forgiveness, goodness, kindness, love, thankfulness, and gratitude.

Do you know who your enemy is? It's your own stinky thinking and your own inner thoughts. This is true for all of us. Learn new and more empowering thoughts and eliminate negative thinking for a better life.

Change your thoughts about yourself, about others, and about whatever you think is upsetting you. Why? *You* are upsetting *you* through your own stinking thoughts. It's what *you* are thinking, or the way *you* are thinking about it that is the issue.

Challenge yourself: When you start to say something negative, or catch yourself saying something negative, stop and ask yourself how you could rephrase that thought in a more positive way. (This takes a little work, but it is well worth the effort.)

Our bodies respond to feelings and impulses that are generated by our thoughts and minds through our thinking process. Your thinking and creative wrongful thoughts create the messes and errors in your life. Therefore, do not blame others when you think negatively or wrongfully and do wrong.

If you continue to focus on problems through your thoughts, you will weigh yourself down into misery with your burdens. Help yourself by overriding all negative thinking and thoughts.

Fix your thoughts on God and heavenly things to lighten your load, and fill your mind with positive, loving thoughts. Get your heart, focus, and mind right.

By the thoughts we think, we create the lives we live every moment, every minute, every hour, every day, every week, every month, and every year whether they are of sorrow, unhappiness, and sadness, or lives of happiness, goodness, and joyfulness.

Change your perception about your situation so you can have better experiences and a better life.

The gifts of joy, or the gifts of hurt, come through your thinking. Your thoughts create your feelings, your reality, your joy, your hurts, your hate, your pain, your depth of love, or lack of love.

We can reveal our deepest thoughts, good or bad, to God and ask Him for His help in a specific way or in a general way. "Ask, and it shall be given you; seek, and ye shall find; knock, and it (the door) shall be opened to you: For every one that asketh receiveth; and he that seeketh findeth; and to him that knocketh it shall be opened" (Matthew 7:7-8 KJV).

Every one of us is accountable before God for our thoughts, behaviors, actions, deeds, motives, attitudes, and speech, as well as the lack of our actions and deeds, or the lack of our uplifting speech to others.

Yes, you and I are individually responsible for how we live our lives before God, before others, and unto ourselves. Give God your focus and all your thoughts. He knows your thoughts and who you are anyway.

Painful situations can bring us down in life; pain can teach us. We can turn our painful experiences into purpose if we take control of our thoughts (mind and feelings) and use the pain to grow and push forward.

Perform no more careless, reckless, neglectful, and hypocritical actions; this is living wrongly. Replace the ugly with the opposite, and live righteously, so you can travel a better highway in your thoughts, mind, heart, and soul, and in this life.

When one continues to look on the dark side of life, situations, circumstances, and conditions, life does not change for the better. Reverse the negative and bad thoughts and behaviors into doing good for God and others to create good thoughts and behaviors. Become a warrior of God's goodness. Only God has all the answers. And Satan is behind our negative thinking.

Changing your focus can change your life.

Your thinking can also create happiness and beautiful thoughts for a beautiful, fulfilled life.

It is our thoughts, minds, and hearts that feed us our hurts and pain in life, as well as the good and love. Do *not* forfeit your opportunity to serve God with praise and thanksgiving and to be happy.

Pastor Talbot Davis at Good Shepherd Church in Charlotte, North Carolina, has said, "Where your mind dwells determine how your life goes." This is very true.

Adjust your thoughts continually to focus on heavenly things just as you continue to adjust the steering of your car while you're driving to stay within the proper lane. Notice that you are continually moving your steering wheel to manage your vehicle. That's the way it is in daily life. You must continually adjust your thoughts and actions to stay on track as you strive to live an obedient and a godly life.

Stop all possible sinful thoughts and conversations before someone gets hurt or gets scarred.

All problems lie in our hearts and minds, *not* outside of our hearts, minds, and thoughts. It is in our mind, thoughts, and hearts where our hurts take place.

Good or bad, if you let your thoughts take control, instead of you controlling your thoughts, your mind and body will follow the direction of those thoughts. Strive for thought control. Right thoughts passing through our minds empower self-restraint.

Our thoughts create our behaviors, and our actions tell others the truth about us. Become the manager of your thoughts so your thoughts don't manage you.

Replace your negative behavior and actions with positive behaviors and actions to enhance and improve your life's outcome.

Mend small conflicts by forgiving any wrongdoing right away, striving for peace.

When you find yourself saying (or thinking) something in a negative way, stop and remember to rephrase what you were saying. Replace your worrisome and negative thinking in a positive way with positive thoughts and words.

Put away your anxious thoughts and trust God always. One cannot worry and trust at the same time.

Give without *thought* of gain. Be sincere in whatever you do. Walk in the way of Jesus and in his footsteps.

Rearrange your priorities in accordance with God's will. Let God stir your heart and soul. Give careful *thought* to your ways of living.

Lessen your wandering, sinful, and judgmental thoughts and turn them over to God, into His presence.

God often shows us that there are more options available than we have thought. Do the right thing, always.

THE HEART

Integrity and maturity are vital to our hearts, souls, and minds.

The mouth speaks when the heart is full of things.

God is interested in you and your heart's desire. He wants what's best for you. Keep up the nourishment of your heart, mind, body, and soul through God's word and love.

"Where your treasure is, there your heart will be also" (Matthew 6:21 NIV).

Without Jesus Christ in our hearts, minds, souls, and lives our vision and hopes are very blurred. Divine guidance prepares our hearts for eternal life. We need hearts of love, and changed souls, and changed minds.

What are you nursing in your heart, mind, and thoughts day after day? Good or unhealthy thoughts?

Jesus says our speech and actions rule our true beliefs. And whatever is stored up in our hearts—good brings good and evil brings evil according to what's in our hearts (see Luke 6:45 NIV).

Live with daily spiritual freshness in your heart and allow it to spread to others.

Brace yourself because the dark days are here to stay and will grow worse unless we change our ways. Set your heart and mind on God and be prepared.

Are you hardening your heart – I pray you're not? On the other hand, are you softening your heart with love, joy, peace, kindness, forgiveness, and servanthood?

In the Bible, a servant is one who voluntarily chose to serve others and displays humility.

The main reason you and I sin daily is that you and I aren't honoring and loving God's first commandment: to love Him with all our hearts, with all our souls, with all our minds, and with all our strength. And we aren't loving one another as we love ourselves. To love God and other people is more important than all offerings and sacrifices (see Mark 12:30–33). There is no other commandment greater than these.

Jesus will lift you up if you call on Him. The peace of God will guard your heart and mind. "Let the peace of Christ rule your heart… you were called to peace. And be thankful. Let the message of Christ dwell among you richly as you teach and admonish one another with all wisdom through psalms, hymns, and songs from the Spirit, singing to God with gratitude in your hearts" (Colossians 3:15–16 NIV).

God wants our hearts—yours and mine. And God wants our light to shine. Grow the beauty of holiness inside your heart, soul, and mind. Do *not* follow the evil of your heart.

Honesty gives us peace that guards our minds and hearts. It is in our hearts where the real power and allegiance lies and leads the way to Jesus Christ.

The truly rich are people who possess *kind hearts*. Your soul will never be happy or satisfied until you have God in your heart and mind. Say with a full, humble heart, "Lord God I am ready for you to direct me and my life."

It is in our heart that evil lies. Sensitivity and submission to God's Word can soften your heart.

For us to stay safe from the devil, we are required to repent and to give full forgiveness to others from our hearts.

Let whatever is in your heart, mind, and soul come spilling out of you when you are talking to Jesus. It is going to come spilling out anyway, so share it with Jesus.

It does not mean you are broken even though your heart is breaking. Allow God to restore your broken heart and keep you on the path of victory. Allow your soul and heart to burn for Jesus Christ and for the truth of the scripture.

OUR SAVIOR JESUS CHRIST

Jesus came to rescue you and me. Have you allowed Him to rescue you?

Jesus came to earth in our image, and we, as believers, are to become like Jesus' spiritual image. Jesus Christ alone is your hope and security. Strengthen your faith in who He is.

Jesus Christ and His Heavenly Father are our best teachers. They give wisdom freely to all who ask.

Humans sacrifice others in many areas for themselves, while Christ sacrificed Himself for us.

The true purpose and meaning in life are *only* found in Jesus! Let Jesus Christ cleanse you. Allow Jesus' love to navigate your life.

Jesus is the head of the church. Let Him be the head over you. The only gift we need is Jesus, for He will fulfill our needs if we pursue Him.

The ruler is Jesus Christ, our Messiah, our Lord, and our Father. Jesus is extremely significant to you and the whole universe! We must learn and realize just how significant He really is to our world and to us.

Jesus never hurt anyone. Practice living as Jesus lived. The Lord is good. He cares for those who trust in Him.

Our spiritual identities come from Jesus. No problem is too big for Jesus' ability. Jesus provides the joy of salvation.

Jesus allowed himself to be crucified and buried. Then, He was resurrected so that He could resurrect you and me out of our graves after our earthly deaths.

Pastor Talbot Davis of Good Shepherd Church in Charlotte, North Carolina, has said, "You can stay in your own self-destructive grave, or you can allow Jesus to bring you out of your grave—your choice."

Jesus is the finest gem! He lived for you and me. He died for you and me. He was resurrected for you and me. He will return for you and me if we endure as servants of Jesus.

"There ain't no grave gonna hold my body down. When I hear the trumpet sound, I'm gonna to rise up out of the ground" (song attributed to Claude Ely).

Jesus said, "Peace I leave you; my peace I give you. I do not give to you as the world gives. Do not let your hearts be troubled and do not be afraid" (John 14:27 NIV).

When we discover who Jesus is and accept His ways, He changes who we are. Christ died for us and did what we cannot do for ourselves.

Jesus Christ will usher in peace during the Millennium throughout the world when He returns as a victorious King (see Revelations 20:6 NIV).

By being a disciple of Jesus, He will bring you out of the grave you stepped into. We need to thrive in following Jesus Christ and obeying Him.

We are power*less* without Jesus Christ. We are to encourage others in truth and faith.

Make every effort to have the ability through Christ to manifest virtue, knowledge, self-control, perseverance, godliness, mutual affection (kindness and compassion), and love. (see 2 Peter 1:5–7 NIV)

Jesus was, and is the Lord God Almighty and is to return as the King of all things (see Revelation 4:8 NIV). He is the Ruler, "King of Kings and Lord of Lords" (1 Timothy 6:15 NIV; see Revelation 17:14 NIV and 19:16 NIV).

Jesus is the Messiah, the Christ! Jesus is the king of our lives. If He's not the king of your life, make Him your king.

We are to be honest because God is truth—nothing but truth. We are to be like Jesus, God's Son. Have purity and let Jesus redeem you from the hand of wickedness.

Only Christ can heal the disease of sin. Jesus has authority to forgive all sins. We do not have the ability to cure ourselves. Only Christ has that ability. Allow Christ to cure your disease of sin.

He provided us with a fuller understanding of why the laws were made in the first place. We are not to live by our own beliefs, but by God's Word.

Don't miss the point of God's laws. Jesus made it clear that obeying and living God's commands (laws) is more important than telling and explaining them to others.

Jesus came to save people regardless of their sins. Continue your efforts to stay true to God. Jesus is our wonderful partner and our savior.

The true God will prevail. Seek God first and foremost. Have no other gods, or idols, before you. God alone is to be worshiped.

We are very fortunate that Jesus clearly revealed to us God, His truth, and how we can know Him.

To be a friend of Jesus, you must be honest with yourself, with others, and with Jesus Christ. You must believe that the Virgin Mary gave birth to Jesus. You must believe in Jesus' death, His resurrection, and His ascension into heaven. You must be a follower of Jesus; and you must believe that He is your savior, the Lord Jesus Christ, who will return like a thief in the night.

Jesus is a friend to people who are willing to admit that they have issues and can't fix them without His help, and to people who are willing to repent of their sins.

Christ is our justifier. Jesus believes we are worthy of being justified if we follow Him faithfully. We are to conform to the image of God's son, Jesus.

Jesus is our shepherd, looking after us for our own good. Jesus wants us to live for Him and one another, *not* for ourselves.

"My sheep listen to my voice; I know them, and they follow me" (John 10:27 NIV).

Jesus demonstrated the greatest humility of all. Jesus was born to teach us how to live and how to find salvation.

Jesus is our hero. Be victorious in whatever you do for Jesus. Jesus Christ is our true eternal hope and savior, regardless of what happens in the world.

"Our citizenship is in heaven. And we eagerly await a Savior from there, the Lord Jesus Christ, who, by the power... will transform our lowly bodies so that they will be like His glorious body" (Philippians 3:20–21 NIV).

"Very truly I tell you, whoever hears my word and believes Him who sent me has eternal life and will not be judged but has crossed over from death to life" (John 5:24 NIV).

Jesus offered us a new way of living and access to God. Jesus gives us hope. He knows the way we need to go. Listen and obey God's Holy Spirit's voice and nudges. Jesus is the Holy Spirit of influence.

Jesus lived a life of impeccable integrity. Jesus was driven by purpose.

He gives you strength and fulfills your needs as He watches over you. Jesus provides us with everything. And Jesus surrounds us every moment of every day.

"I am the living bread that came down from heaven. Whoever eats this bread will live forever. This bread is my flesh, which I will give for the life of the world" (John 6:51 NIV).

If Jesus knocks on the door of your soul, welcome Him in. Jesus sacrificed Himself to reconcile us to God. Jesus is the doorkeeper of Heaven.

Jesus Christ thought of others first. He placed all of us first; therefore, we need to place Jesus Christ and others before ourselves.

He forgives us if we repent and confess our sins. Repent and live life by doing better. Do not repeat bad behavior.

Jesus is the brightness and the light of your life and my life. He is involved in all the good you and I experience.

The Lord's Supper (communion) is a time to look backward and to look forward. Jesus is returning someday.

Jesus promises never to leave us or forsake us. However, we can leave Him. I wouldn't advise you to do that. Keep your eternal home in mind always.

Jesus gave up His spirit on the cross for us. (see Matthew 27:50 NIV)

Jesus came to earth and died our deaths so that we could have eternal life as Christians if we take His righteous path.

"Following Jesus does not exempt you from suffering, it sustains you through it." [1]Devin Tharp

He provides so we may proclaim His prize of eternal life, joy, and love. Make Jesus Christ your focal point.

"The earth will be filled with the knowledge of the Lord" (Isaiah 11:9 NIV).

Jesus loves everyone but hates their evil and *all* wrong doings.

"Look to the Lord and His strength; seek His face always" (Psalm 105:4 NIV).

---

[1] 1 Devin Tharp, "God and the Broken-Hearted," Good Shepherd Church, February 14, 2020.

OUR MIRACULOUS GOD

We love our children deeply, but we do not approve of their wrongs. God loves us, and He does not approve of our wrongs.

The Holy Spirit gives us power, strength, love, guidance, and discipline within. Christ gives us the power to overcome sin. You and I can endure when God empowers us, and His power heals us.

"His divine power has given us everything we need for a godly life through our knowledge of Him who called us by His own glory and goodness" (2 Peter 1:3 NIV).

Join the work of God's cavalry. Without God, there is no hope or comfort. Hope is knowing God and resting in His love. God's word tells us He can provide us shelter from all temptations.

At all times, we have access to God's presence because Jesus died for us so we could have direct access to God.

Let the Lord be with you no matter what life brings. Let God comfort you.

Let's get out and do what God has in mind for us to do. God has given us jobs to do. And that is helping to change the world for Him, and with Him. Only through God's spirit can we succeed. God expects us to trust Him no matter what.

God gives us resources and things to manage here on earth in preparation for our future tasks in heaven.

Let your standards be those written in God's Word that God presented to us. God does not want words; He wants right behavior and actions. God cannot be deceived.

The same God who created you can be trusted with your life, but only when you trust Him. It is better to obey God than to defy Him. Run toward God, not away from Him.

What God wants is to restore us from our sin and rebellion. He loves us and wants us to love and obey Him.

God loves perfectly and completely. Ask God to keep your heart open and full of love, and to help you stay sensitive to others who need help and kindness.

God chose to do His work through His people, and God provides us the resources to do His work. God loves to be trusted. Allow God to motivate you to witness for Him.

God is the God Almighty, the Holy Creator, and the King of kings whose name is above every name.

"Restore us to yourself, Lord, that we may return; renew our days as of old" (Lamentations 5:21 NIV).

Always acknowledge God as your Lord and God. Worship God for who He is: the Creator of all things. He rules everything inside and outside of this world. He is the *God* of the *whole universe.*

God's compassions never fail. His mercies are renewed every morning. (see Lamentations 3:22–23 NIV)

If you want to be happy, draw close to God. He is the source of happiness. He wants the best for you. God values you.

God disciplines His children to keep them from going astray by using afflictions to bring us back to Him because God wants to cleanse our lives—yours and mine.

God tries to purify us through troublesome and difficult circumstances and situations. He desires us to turn to Him and cling to Him during these times.

God is a provider who is limit*less*, and a protector who is *all-powerful.* His Word and promises are *un*changing.

God is a prayer answerer, miracle worker, and healer.

Allow God to guard your life. Never forget that God keeps His word, so you should keep yours.

God has given us the power of restraint. Ask the Holy Spirit to activate His power within you. Nothing is better than God-strength!

God's power can transform you and me. God governs the world according to His purposes.

God helps us to stop our sorrowfulness and variety of griefs so that we can focus on His greatness and glorious power.

God does not have a body like you or me. God is Spirit. He never changes. He is never changing.

"Heaven and earth will pass away, but my words will never pass away" (Luke 21: 33 NIV).

Every promise in the Bible will come to pass. God's eternal punishment will come to pass also. Be assured of these promises of His.

You and I absolutely can count on God because He will not deceive you, and He does not and cannot lie.

"Every good and perfect gift is from above" (James 1:17 NIV), from our Heavenly Father.

> God is absolutely pure!
> God is absolutely holy!
> God *cannot* accept sin!

God has given you and me magnificent gifts: His Son and a chance for eternal life.

Recognize and know that God is always in control! God holds all power in His hands. God's plans are unshakable.

God can help you to create boldness and beauty in your mind, heart, soul, and life.

God is in us if we are believers. His Holy Spirit dwells within each Christian.

God renews and refreshes His daily provisions every morning for all people.

Be confident in God's final victory! He is the God of the universe! We can trust Him.

Only God can provide true security! God demands complete justice and fair*ness*.

God is displeased with rebellion, inward and outward, as well as arrogance, pride, envy, and dishonesty. Let go of all these evil behaviors.

God is the Source and all our power and strength comes from God. Only God Himself can satisfy the deep longings (holes) of one's soul.

God has an agenda for us to follow. The agenda is found in the Bible. God is not pleased with us when we isolate ourselves from others' needs. God wants us to stay focused and motivated to help other souls. God rejoices when we do right, and He rejoices in what we do for Him.

God wants us to acknowledge Him, worship Him as the Creator, glorify Him, and praise Him. Acquire new habits and a higher relationship with God. God examines everyone.

Put Christ in every aspect of your life. God is with you through your most challenging circumstances and through the good times. Everywhere and always, your God is there, present and watching!

God has been present forever, "from of old, from ancient times" (Micah 5:2 NIV).

"God is the King of all the earth; sing to him a psalm of praise" (Psalm 47:7 NIV). Because God is Holy.

Pastor Talbot Davis of Good Shepherd Church in Charlotte, North Carolina, has said, "God is your charger when you have a low battery."

God has never seen a problem too big. No matter what the problems are, they're not too big or too much for God's authority.

God is not temporary. He is our dwelling place. Let God work in your life.

God is concerned about every human being, and we believers need to be concerned for people also. God is everywhere, unlimited, and all-powerful. "With God all things are possible" (Matthew 19:26 NIV).

God is eternal. God always was, always is, and always will be. (see Revelation 4:8 NIV)

God's help is available as we strive to follow Jesus, even when we feel we don't deserve it. God is the provider of all our abilities. God and His strength are perfect for us to lean on continually. Walk in the shadow of His protection.

God is far greater than we can comprehend. God has no peers. There is only one God. God is *superior* to *all* things. God opened the way for us to have eternal life through Jesus Christ and His crucifixion.

God is with us to meet our present needs. Nothing at all is impossible for Him, our Almighty Lord. The battle belongs to the Lord. God will deliver all His people from all the world powers that oppress them. We are going to see victory.

God is ahead of us and beckoning us forward in following Him. The best is yet to be. He is Lord of all people. We are called to honor God's name and to obey all of God's laws.

When God restores us, it will be a day of rejoicing. We'll see things differently when our hearts have been reconciled and cleansed by God.

It is *im*possible to escape God. God is everywhere! Lean on His truth as your crutch. Every day, allow God to renew you. God's trust is like a staff that you can lean on.

God Almighty is the artist of the beauty on, in, and around this earth: galaxies, stars, landscapes, the light and darkness, shadows, and flakes of snow that create a spectacular white blanket to cover the drab of winter with wonderment. He is all-powerful, gentle, kind, and loving through His daily blessings. Be thankful for all of God's provisions daily.

God certainly has the wisdom and knowledge of all things from heaven above to down under. He knows everything that's going on everywhere and in all people.

God created life in you and me, but you and I get to choose and decide how to fill that life: with love or evil. I *don't suggest* that you fill your life doing *evil*. I strongly encourage you *not* to invite evil into your life. *Fill your life with good words and good deeds*. Honoring God.

As children of God, God is our ever-present helper. He protects us and watches over our lives.

God tests us to know what's in our hearts, and He strengthens us also. All wisdom comes from God above.

God created us with amazing abilities and compatibility; therefore, we need to keep our focus on doing whatever is required for us to live eternal lives with our Lord Jesus Christ.

God can provide you what you need and can help you to gain perspective. He has the power. He is in control.

God is the most generous person in all creation. God loved us so very much that He gave us His only begotten son so we could have an eternal life of love and peace forevermore. (see John 3:16 NIV)

"You, Lord, are forgiving and good, abounding in love to all who call to you" (Psalm 86:5 NIV).

All that God says is sure to happen! It will happen! Most of what God said has already come about.

God provides us ways to escape every wrong thing. Usually, it appears when we start going in the wrong direction. Immediately take the escape route always. Remember to listen to the nudges that the Holy Spirit is providing you. With no hesitation, take the escape.

Our passionate God can change the course of our lives. Change whatever needs to be changed in your life for the glory of God.

God has been exceedingly patient with us. He has given us many opportunities to turn to Him. God wants us to be merciful, humble, just, and fair.

"I said, 'You are my servant'; I have chosen you and have not rejected you. So do not fear, for I am with you; do not be dismayed, for I am your God. I will strengthen you and help you; I will uphold you with my righteous right hand" (Isaiah 41:9b–10 NIV).

God made a way for us to fully live joyful lives. God is with us always, until the end of the world.

Bring honor and glory to our Lord God, Jesus Christ.

OUR TEMPLE

We are the creators of our choices. How we build our thoughts affects our temples—*not only* our own temples (lives) *but* other people's temples (lives) as well.

We need to take Jesus Christ seriously. We need to begin supporting our personal temples with love and caring behavior while being servants of God and doing all we can to be ready when the end comes.

Our bodies are temples for the Holy Spirit to dwell in. Our job is to let the world see Jesus in our temples.

We are the keepers and builders of our own personal temples that have been given to us by God. Since your body is God's temple, make sure you keep it clean and holy. Do not defile it.

We are children of God, so Satan has no place in us. But know your faith (temple) framework is inadequate without the Lord directing you.

Do not let others see Satan in you or invite Satan into your temple. We must recognize our own sinfulness. Invite God into your temple to stay forever.

STANDARDS TO LIVE BY

Don't let anyone or anything seduce you into lowering your standards, compromising your moral principles, and turning away from God.

Anyone who accepts the standards of God and is willing to obey Him may enjoy the blessings of God's rules.

Living what you know that's good is a lot more meaningful than just having knowledge.

Our conduct, behaviors, and actions speak much louder than what we say. Examine and compare your actions and motives with God's standards.

Be faithful and devoted wholeheartedly to God daily. Empty yourself of fleshly desires and fill yourself with spiritual desires. Obey God, no matter what the rest of the world does.

Christ-like love is the key. Love needs to navigate our lives.

Select a verse, or a few verses, to ponder each morning. Let the verse(s) guide you through your day.

Be faithful to God - our Lord Jesus Christ, yourself, your spouse, family, friends, and others as well as being truthful at all times.

Obey the Ten Commandments and God's commands. Jesus did not do away with the laws.

Decide to stop complaining and weeping over what you can't do and begin to glorify and worship God through what you can do. Aspire to please God using your gifts, talents, and abilities so that pleasing God will become a desire within your heart also. Everything from God is good.

THOUGHTS ON LOVE

God has a way to overcome obstacles. It's called *love*. Love everyone. Even if you think you wouldn't like them, show love to them.

Jesus encourages, loves, and forgives, and we need to do the same.

Be emptied of self and fill your mind with scripture to build a deeper love for everyone. Always show love and forgiveness even when it is hard. Show love and compassion in your actions.

Your love is mighty and unlimited. The more love you give away, the more love you have. Live a life that reaps good things, including an eternal life of love and joy.

We must put away our indifference about God's requirements and love one another, be obedient, be faithful to Him and to others, and produce good fruit.

We are taught how to love by the greatest authority of all: Jesus Christ. However, our love is a speck in the dust compared to God's great love.

The greatest love story: "For God so loved the world, that he gave his only begotten Son, that whosoever believeth in him should not perish, but have everlasting life" (John 3:16 KJV).

How do we please and show God our love? We need to do this by dying to this world, showing love and mercy to all people through our hearts, helping and giving to others, serving Him with a servant's heart, repenting, praying, praising God, reading the Bible daily, worshipping Him and living as His disciples. This is how we please God and show God, we love Him.

Parents' rules show their love for their children. The same is true for God's rules. He loves you.

To glorify God, we must strive to love God and one another more fully and deeper than we love ourselves. We need to do for others as we do for our own selves.

Do not let what you have accomplished defeat your next achievement for God. Why? We are to continually proclaim Jesus' love in words and actions to the whole world.

Godly indicators are love, joy, peace, patience, gentleness, kindness, goodness, meekness, faithfulness, self-restraint, and longsuffering (see Galatians 5:22–23). These are the fruits of the spirit and servanthood. God wants our light and fruits to reflect these behaviors while we say no to our carnal nature.

Learn what the spiritual priorities are from the Word of God. Love God with all your strength, mind, heart, body, and soul, and love others as you love yourself—only better. And have love for all people but hate their evil and wicked ways.

Fix your eyes, ears, and hearts on what is unseen, but everlasting. Focus on God's love. See God's love in all things.

Be grounded and rooted in God's love as you pattern your lives on how Jesus lived His life, and as He taught His disciples and others to live.

Our goal is to love according to Jesus' image and hopefully become like the person Jesus was and is, not living according to the current circumstances or according to another person.

When you *don't know what to do, answer with gestures of love: hugs, smiles,* and *nice surprises.* Express love in some way. Love will get you through.

When we work for God, God works for us, showing us His love, goodness, gifts, blessings, and rewards.

Our success is not from ourselves. It is from the all-powerful God. He gives us our strength, wisdom, knowledge, and the know-how. Why? Because He loves us. Trust God always!

Listen to God and respond. God's love remains steadfast. There are boundless treasures in our Lord Christ's unchanging love.

The cost of being Christ's disciple—believing, striving, and following God and His Word—is worth the value of having an eternal home and a life of love forevermore. The reward is much greater than we can ever imagine.

What we must give up and have to give up for being Christians is of little importance compared to what we will gain if we are believers: eternal life with Christ Jesus, living in heaven in pure love.

It is possible to follow God consistently with His transforming love in our hearts.

God gives us the greatest kindness. He loves us with an everlasting love—unconditional pure love—agape love.

God provides and supplies us with many gifts. These include grace, mercy, the Holy Spirit, a conscience, feelings, free will, choices, and the faculties of our minds (reason, memory, creativity, imagination, perception, will, and thoughts). His gifts also include light, darkness, air, oxygen, breath, healings, sight, hearing, feet, motion, sensations, smell, taste, speech and many more gifts. He provides us the ability to travel and enjoy miraculous wonders and beauty in all variations and forms. We need to welcome and receive them with gratitude to the most glorious Holy God, who is the creator of life and of everything above and below. He is a magnificent and inexhaustible God without end.

God demonstrated His true, genuine (*agape*) love, for us when He sent His only Son as a baby born in a manger on earth and allowed Him to be sacrificed on the cross for *all* our sins.

God is the same Almighty God who gives us His forgiveness, love, mercy, grace, peace, and the Holy Spirit to guide our way, keeping us on the narrow righteous path of love, mercy, grace, and forgiveness.

The reason each person sin (including myself) is that he or she isn't keeping God's first two commandments. The first is to love God with *all of* your heart, *with all your* soul, with *all* of your mind, and with all of your strength. The second is to love others as yourself. We are failing in loving God and others the way God intended.

Clothe yourself in love, praise, encouragement, hope, and prayer every day.

When you focus on a relationship with God, you will start to sprout and grow, like a healthy plant, in His Word and love. You will then produce greater harvests of love, kindness, goodness, patience, and self-control, and minister to others because of your growth and maturity in God.

God's love is a love of action. Be the salt of love, of kindness, and of God's message in the world. We have a responsibility to obey, love, and protect ourselves and others.

To ignore the poor is to ignore those whom God loves. God wants us to reach out to help others. Treat the poor and oppressed with kindness, love, and compassion.

Remember to treat people with love, kindness, goodness, patience, gentleness, and with self-control.

Plan your eternal future with purpose for a rich welcome from Jesus Christ our Lord. Live your life well. His love endures forever.

How we live and what we give and show others (our mates, parents, siblings, friends, co-workers, strangers) reflects the sincerity of our relationship with God, and hopefully we show love to them.

The standards for honesty, integrity, love, and compassion come from God, *not* society.

Distinguish yourself from others by showing greater love to others.

Live by faith. Let God intervene. Listen and trust God. He is real! Let the power of God's grace and love be your finish line.

There will be a never-ending supply of God's love, wisdom, understanding, knowledge, serving, encouraging, forgivingness, mercy, and grace.

Bring the freshness of God's power and love to your life, and into others' lives. Forgive one another and let love mend and heal you.

Don't forget who gave you your life, and do *not* turn away from the one who truly loves you: God Himself. Let God and hope carry you in and through difficult times.

Focus on loving and being honest and dwell constantly on Jesus Christ and His love so evil can't win.

Let God's love be your guide. Live for God so that you will live forever in joy and love. Be devoted to God's desires and show your love and mercy to the world.

Create a desire for God's pardon and love.

Don't chase happiness that doesn't last. Chase God and His blessings, and true happiness, joy, and love will enter into your life as you love God and help others.

Allow your heart and eyes to see the provisions that God provides, and your eyes and ears to be sensitive to the voice of God's joy and deliverance as you serve God as His servant in love.

"Follow God's example, therefore, as dearly loved children and walk in the way of love, just as Christ loved us and gave Himself up for us as a fragrant offering and sacrifice to God" (Ephesians 5:1–2 NIV).

FOLLOWERS / BELIEVERS

According to the apostle Paul, we have been chosen, adopted, accepted, redeemed, enlightened, given an inheritance, sealed, secured, and forgiven, (see Ephesians 1:4–14 NIV) if we are born again. And if we are children believing in the Heavenly Father and in Christ Jesus, and if we stay faithful to Him, we are guaranteed a citizenship because we have been chosen and adopted as His children.

Set your hearts and sights on the realities of Heaven. (see Colossians 3:1 NIV)

Your sins have been paid for you if you are a true follower of Jesus. God blots out His followers' transgressions for His own sake and remembers our sins no more. (see Isaiah 43:25)

Christians, let us live as forgiven people. As believers, our souls never die.

If you accept God as your Father and become a follower, He will meet your spiritual needs and fill your soul to stop the longings.

Be willing to carry out the responsibility God gives you. As believers, we must do what God tells us to do.

The cost of less free time, giving up bad habits, lost popularity, lost friendships, and whatever else is necessary for us to be a follower of Jesus Christ is worth the cost we must pay to live as believers and followers of Jesus Christ our Lord.

Jesus is preparing a place for us in His Father's house. He will come back and take us to be with Him (see John 14:1-3) so that we will be where He is forevermore.

Take the Christian walk seriously. The law for Christian living is forward, not backward. Be onward bound as a faithful servant.

The Christian life is about loving one another: assisting others, encouraging them, supporting them, visiting them, and praying with them and for oneself. And the place for Christians is their local churches.

One of the qualities of a Christian is generosity. Generosity is about what's in our hearts. If you're not generous, ask God to help you to show generosity to Him and others.

You can't be a part-time Christian. It's not enough. Listen to the Lord. Do not be deceived. Get excited about God. Honor God.

Do not compromise Christian principles. We are to follow Jesus' ways and God's Word, the Bible. A Christian life requires a sustained determination. Endurance is needed.

As Christians and God's disciples, we are to become disciplined according to the teaching of our Lord Jesus Christ. Be true and follow God. Do not follow the world's practices.

Continue to strengthen your faith in God daily by reading His Word. We need faith to live as followers of Jesus and to continue living Christian lives.

Always see your potential in God's eyes because God sees all Christians' great potential.

Keeping oaths and promises are very important! Are you known as a person of your word? As a child of God? As a Christian?

There is a mark, a target, a goal, and a standard God established as ungodly (as sin); there is also a godly mark, a target, and a goal for true followers and believers in God and His holiness.

If a person becomes a Christian, Christ will take the person's clothes of sin and replace them with God's clothes of righteousness.

As Christians, we have no need to fear or be dismayed for Jesus is with us. We can feel very secure in God and His love and power. He is your God and mine. He will strengthen us because He has not rejected us.

There will be a never-ending supply of God's love, mercy, forgiveness, and cleansing for the Christian, the child of God.

Trusting and obeying God and living for God protects you from being condemned and ending up in hell.

A disciple is a follower of Christ. As disciples, we are to take on Jesus' priorities as our own. His desires become our desires. His agenda becomes our agenda.

The apostle Paul said, "Follow my example, as I follow the example of Christ" (1 Corinthians 11:1 NIV).

Jesus' death redeemed believers from the bondage of sin and death.

As Christians, we need to emphasize our faith by continually showing compassion, love, and forgiveness to all people, including any enemies and anyone we despise.

"Whoever pursues righteousness and love finds life, prosperity and honor" (Proverbs 21:21 NIV).

BE WILLING TO...

Be willing to let there be no divisions between us. (see 1 Corinthians 1:10 NIV)

Be willing to let only good come out of your mouth: praise, truth, thankfulness, uplifting words, and encouraging words.

Be willing to "Watch out for false prophets" (Matthew 7:15 NIV).

Be willing to get back to God's original purpose. Be God-centered, not self-centered.

Be willing to always show the true expression of the church: Jesus Christ.

Be willing to let the beauty of Christ glow in you and from you.

Be willing to change your life by looking to the light. Jesus is our shining light.

Be willing to prepare to see God's work as you prepare for the return of Jesus Christ.

Be willing to be righteous and live by faith.

Be willing to tell others about Christ with all the wisdom God has given you. (see Colossians 1:28 NIV)

Be willing to let His life and light shine in you. Shine your light to the rest of the world.

Be willing to have a trusting attitude that God is with you, whether you sense His presence or not.

Be willing to listen to the spiritual counsel of others and to God's words.

Be willing to develop a stronger spiritual life by looking to God during both the good and bad times.

Be willing to have spiritual integrity and practice heartfelt obedience toward God our Lord.

Be willing to converse with God throughout your day.

Be willing to push back on the demands of your day and spend time with God, your Father.

Be willing to enjoy the banquet God has prepared before you.

Be willing to align yourself with God's perspectives and commands. Be receptive to God.

Be willing to trust God regardless of what is happening in your life, or whatever is happening around you.

Be willing to separate yourselves from the ungodliness of wickedness and wrong, sinful behavior. Yield to God and follow His laws and ways.

Be willing to allow your life to bring honor to your bridegroom, the Lord.

Be willing to learn and know what your purpose is as a Christian living for Jesus Christ.

Be willing to let God work through you. We are His hands and feet on earth. Keep your focus on His will.

Be willing to never forget God is Holy and never approach God carelessly.

Be willing to *not* become inactive and defeat your next great achievement in life.

Be willing to put Him *first*. Let God provide your deepest needs. Where is God on your priority list?

Be willing to make God, the highest platform, your dwelling place.

Be willing to keep God's word and to keep your word.

Be willing to make a firm commitment to God. Obeying God is the way to find fulfillment and satisfaction in your life.

Be willing to stand firm in God's limit*less* power and His promises when you're facing impossible odds.

Be willing to do your best! If you are doing, you have started.

Be willing to live for God. Life is better with us living as children of God.

Be willing to stay in agreement with God. Our beliefs make a difference in our lives. God knows best.

Be willing to live with confidence as a believer. God knows everything about you. Do not lose sight of God. Seek His presence.

Be willing to proclaim God to the world.

SIN – WHAT IS SIN?

Sin leads all humans in the wrong direction—from love and truth to corruption and rebellion.

Sin affects our minds and hearts as well as other people in a negative way.

Sin affects our perception and our perspective.

God allowed Jesus, His son, to die on the cross and shed His blood so we could be cleansed of our sins.

God does *not* like our complaints, grumbling, slandering, cursing, gossiping, and the like. These behaviors are sins.

Thankfulness keeps you from criticizing, gossiping, talking negatively, and complaining; these are sins.

Take every necessary action to get rid of sin and anything that causes you to sin, regardless of what that sin is.

You and I have a choice: obey God and receive blessings or disobey God and face the consequences—the curse of death.

We all need to ask God to help us let go of our sins and our sinful ways, and to show us better ways to live and serve Him.

Each time we purposely sin, we harden our hearts. Sin seems more natural with each repetition. All the while it hardens our hearts more and more away from our eternal life with Jesus Christ.

Many people sin because they have stopped being mindful of their sinful habits. Intentionally be observant of all your behaviors.

If an act is wrong, so is the intention. Separate yourself from the world's sinful values.

Lying is a sin and it's costly. Have sorrow for your sins.

Lying really hurts people. Lying leaves scars, as when a nail is removed, the nail leaves its scar (a hole).

Do not rationalize sin! We are *not* to follow the ways of others or the world.

Call on God. He will give you the strength if you need to escape a sin you are thinking of doing, or that you are currently doing.

Continued sin hardens a person's heart. Steer away from sinful practices and put away your sinful nature.

Do not give in to the pressures of the sinful ways of life around you. Do not accept society's way of life. Accept only Jesus' way of life.

Don't make a mockery of God or worship. We cannot truthfully praise God and willfully sin at the same time.

We must answer to God for how we act and live. We will all have to account for our sins—all of us.

If you are relying on grace to cover your sins, you are in trouble. Grace alone is not enough.

There are no sizes of little, big, or huge sin. Sin is sin. What some people call little white lies, or fibs, aren't those things; they are lies. Do not measure lying by how much damage a lie may do. A lie is a lie, big or tiny, it's still a lie. Sin comes in all sizes from tiny to humongous.

Active worship will *not* clean up our sins; only repentance and obedience can do that.

Put to death the sinful things within you. Replace sin with loving and serving God and His people, His ministry, the church, the poor, the needy, the widows, the elders, the sick, the lonely, and so on.

To God, all sin is equal, and sinners are loveable. God loves everyone. However, just because God loves everyone doesn't mean sinners will go to heaven.

God does not take sin lightly; the person who sins will be punished.

Sin is extremely distasteful to God. And sin is anything that goes against what God wants for us.

God has rules, and if we step outside the obedience boundaries, we are sinning. (Look up *sin* in the dictionary.)

Sin is sin. Wrong is wrong. Hate sin - all evil.

We burden God with our sins and weary Him with our offenses.

Sometimes we sin by omission (e.g., not doing what we need to be doing to please God). Sin hurts us, sin hurts others, our friendships, and our relationships.

Sin should not, and need not, be your master. Life under sin is not true life; it is not worth living. You must be the master over your sin and your thoughts.

Deception can break a good spirit in a single strike. "You may be sure that your sin will find you out" (Numbers 32:23 NIV).

Many people do not understand the depth of their sins. Do you understand the depth of your sins?

Consider the change that needs to take place in your life. Each sin makes the next one easier to commit.

The more one sins, the harder it is to remember what's right, or what God's desires are. This is true for each one of us.

Sin includes not *only* what we do, but what we refuse to do – we don't do. To disobey God is to invite disaster.

What we ignore can cause us to stumble. Withholding help, love, or forgiveness is sin.

Disobedience leads to sin. Wrong attitudes, wrong thoughts, and wrong actions are also sins. Sin and disobedience hurt us and endanger us and others.

Leading others astray, away from God, is one of the worst sins. Do not take God for granted! Embrace justice and God!

Sin was in our hearts when we were born. Also, we learned sin from the world. It's time to destroy sin and break the sin habit.

God alone can save you. Turn from sinning and walk with God.

Every time we sin, we pay a price. What if each time we sinned, we had to make some sacrifice, or offer of money, according to the sin that we committed? Would you sin intentionally if you had to make a payment for your sin?

We will be held responsible for all sins we commit unless we repent sincerely, and are truly sorrowful of our sin, meaning you and I never plan to repeat the sin again.

Knock down that giant of sin standing between you and God. Our sinful nature and strength are hindrances to us.

When strong wrong desires are conceived, the desires give birth to sin. Do not allow your sin to grow by nourishing wrong desires. Intentionally, sin *no* more.

Did you know that lying and murder result in the same spiritual penalty?

According to the Bible, lying is the same as murder and the same as any other great sin. Tell no lies for fewer problems here on earth and live a godly Christian life for an eternal life in heaven.

Lying is evil. The devil "is a liar and the father of lies" (John 8:44 NIV). Lying is a sin and a coward's way of getting out of trouble temporarily. "The cowardly...will be consigned to the fiery lake of burning sulfur. This is the second death." (Revelation 21:8 NIV).

There are seven things God despises and six things He hates (see Proverbs 6). Look at lies as God looks at lies. Lying is false; therefore, it is falsehood and very misleading and deceiving.

God sent Jesus His son to earth to give His life as ransom for our sin, and to heal and carry our burdens and change our lives. Freedom from sin comes only from Christ Jesus.

REPENT

Sincerely repent and ask God to forgive you, then allow Him to help you change your ways and your behavior. Show reverence to God.

No one is beyond the reach of God's forgiveness if the person truly repents, changes his or her ways, and does not continue those sinful deeds. You will receive mercy and forgiveness if you repent and ask God to forgive you.

You are responsible for repenting in order to be forgiven and to have a life with Christ Jesus. God lovingly forgives us when we truly repent and have sincere hearts.

God's punishment for sin is certain. Each time we sin, we reduce our eternal reward. And if you are relying on grace to cover your sins, you are in trouble. Grace alone is not enough.

What should we do with regrets? The words that the Lord gives us is to live the Ten Commandments as well as repent and sin no more.

Repentance means a change in your behavior and speech. No one is beyond redemption! Trust in Him and be saved.

Give up sin, repent and turn (or return) to God. Worship God by following and obeying His Word. God forgives everyone who turns away from sin. Refusing to repent shows we love our sins. Repent and turn from sin today!

Repent and ask God for His forgiveness and help when you realize you have sinned.

Baptism is an outward sign of repentance and forgiveness.

PRIDE

Pride erodes our hearts and destroys relationships, for pride is very destructive.

Pride keeps a person from God. A prideful person thinks he or she doesn't need help or guidance.

Give up pride. No one is exempt from God's justice. Do not let the pride of your heart deceive you. Pride is the surest route to self-destruction. Pride destroys.

A self-sufficient attitude may be our downfall, or pride may be our downfall. Guard yourself and your heart against pride and complacency.

Has pride hardened your heart?

Put pride and being offended aside to make room for love and joy, and display love to all. Everybody matters.

FORGIVENESS

Forgiveness is key to set yourself free from prison, where you are locked up in your own jail (mental hell). Giving forgiveness to the person you haven't forgiven frees you from jail, your mental torment.

Many times, we sin when we focus on ourselves. Ask for forgiveness and turn your attention to God's mission— obeying and focusing on fulfilling God's purpose while focusing on loving and serving others.

What shields are you carrying around? Bitterness, hatred, unforgiveness, and immorality, or love, mercy, grace, forgiveness, compassion, and generosity?

Forgiveness brings joy or peace to the forgiver. Give forgiveness often and freely.

Learn the power of forgiveness by forgiving those who have wronged you.

When Jesus changed the world, He truly forgave!

GOD'S JUDGMENT

To escape God's judgment, we must accept His correction, listen to Him, seek His guidance, and trust Him. God's punishment for our sins is a means of purifying His people.

Believe in God's mighty power and be assured that God's final judgment day is coming. God promises judgment and punishment for all who refuse to follow Him.

The purpose of God's judgment is correction, not revenge. God corrects us as a loving parent would when a child disobeys in rebellion.

God judges a sinful world. The message is clear: disobedience, rebellion, and injustice will not prevail but will be punished severely by our righteous and Holy God, who rules over the full universe, the earth, the heavens, and all creations.

Judgment will come. Sin will *not* go unchecked forever. God will *not* allow sin to continue.

God is coming to rule the earth and judge all people. Plead to God for His mercy and forgiveness. Live your life for Jesus Christ.

"I tell you that everyone will have to give account on the day of judgment for every empty word they have spoken. By your words you will be acquitted, and by your words you will be condemned" (Matthew 12:36-37 NIV).

Judgment is coming upon us. The responsibility is upon each of us individually. Are you prepared for God to speak judgment upon you, your family, and your friends?

Plead to God for Him to be your protector, vindicator, and righteous judge.

Our ways and works will be exposed and examined. Our thoughts, motives, actions, and intentions will be examined. The quality of our work here on earth will not only be examined but judged and exposed.

The Almighty God will judge us according to what our ways and our practices deserve. God will judge us according to the way we treat others. We will be judged according to our hearts, the fruit of our lives, idle words, attitudes, and motives. (see Jeremiah 17:10 NIV, Revelation 2:23 NIV, Matthew 12:36-37 NIV)

If you are judging, you are not loving and serving God.

PRAYER

Never hesitate to ask God for radical change if you will honor Him with the change.

The next time you have a conflict and problems, ask God to help you to gain something beneficial from your problems. Prayer can bring insight, deliverance, and forgiveness.

A lot of things happen when we pray. *Sending sincere prayers up to God creates powerful results and causes miracles to happen.*

God is worthy of our prayers. Praying sincere prayers are how we are to pray.
(My daughter's health is an example of a miracle due to me praying sincerely. My daughter had a brain bleed. As I was getting up from kneeling and praying to God, God said, "She'll be alright." I replied, "God I'm going to trust You that my daughter will be alright." I trusted and had no worries and I felt at peace. Each time as a doctor talked with me, under my breath I was saying, "God, You said she would be alright, and I'm trusting you that she will be alright and that she will have no side effects." She had no side effects. God healed my daughter. She was back surfing within six weeks, after her incision had healed completely.)

"Pray in the Spirit on all occasions with all kinds of prayers and requests. With this in mind, be alert and always keep on praying for all the Lord's people" (Ephesians 6:18 NIV).

"Do not be anxious about anything, but in every situation, by prayer and petition, with thanksgiving, present your requests to God" (Philippians 4:6 NIV).

Prayer is a qualification that matters to God.

Have confidence that God will hear and answer your prayers. However, sometimes the answer doesn't come quickly; weeks, months, or years can pass. Do not become discouraged. Keep praying and believing.

God's answers to prayers may not be what you were expecting, but know His answers are the best for His kingdom and His purpose.

Use the prayer of Daniel (9:4–19) as a prescription for revitalizing your own experience with prayer.

Jesus' prayers were anchored in His Father's promises. Affirm God and His glory. Recognize His mercy. Appeal to God on behalf of others.

Call out to God in earnest prayer. Just a prayer away is God's solution.

Prayer is more effective than worry or panic.

Beg and ask for His forgiveness. You don't need an appointment to call God or to talk to God. He is always available to you any hour of the day or night. So, call on Him to help you in whatever you need whenever you need help.

Ask God to give you the power and strength to be a child of His, and to give you the power and strength to witness to people, and to always let your light shine!

I once heard a minister say something to this effect: For a life-altering experience, when you feel more important, or more competitive, than the other person, begin to pray for more blessings on the other person.

Trust in God, Call upon Him and be saved. God answers prayers.

Offer up prayers to God, allowing Him in your heart, mind, and soul, and allowing Him to guide you. Praise Him daily.

We don't take God as seriously as we need to. Stop focusing on all the rules and start focusing on your relationship with God.

Let God know you are sincere in having a stronger relationship with Him through praying and reading the Bible and other spiritual books. Trust Him for a change and a renewal in your spirit, strength, and courage. Walk with Him, serve Him, and help others as His servant in faith.

Handle life with prayer and continue in prayer with praise and great thanksgiving.

We need to be faithful for a meaningful worship and prayer life. We must learn to move forward on our knees through praying a variety of prayers.

Our position in kneeling is important because it shows our willingness in yielding to God.

When your world is falling apart, run to God and fall on your knees. Be persistent and consistent in prayer.

Pray that the Lord will completely guide you in all things. Pray for those who hurt you. Grow toward maturity and wholeness.

Sentence prayers are very valuable and so are instant prayer that's needed instantly such as: God forgive us. Help me, now! Save us! Guide me, I need you. Guide us daily to you Lord.

Make a wireless call (it's called a prayer) to God whenever you need help, or whenever you need to know what to do. Recognize your need for God's help.

Keep striving in loving and praying. Never stop striving in serving the Lord our God or praying. Prayer confirms hope in God.

Pray that God will give you a heart and eyes to see, and ears to hear with insight into His direction for you.

Reminder: regularly set aside time for God. Pray often throughout each day. Make God and His Word part of your daily life. Strive for holiness.

Hold yourself and your life together with prayer to Jesus Christ as your Heavenly Father.

God values your prayers, and He values you!

Ask God to give you courage to not be bogged down with worry or feeling too low, and to strengthen you in your faith, mind, body, and heart, and to strengthen your discipline and determination.

Ask God to show you new opportunities and ways you can be thankful.

God is giving you breathe and pumping blood through your veins daily, and so much more. Give God the gratitude He deserves.

Call on God and He will give you the prescription and antidote you need for living life when you need it the most.

Ask for God's guidance, then look for it, and then be willing to accept it. Pray: Lord let us all grow in your spiritual wonder and power.

When you are weak or feel stuck, continually ask God to strengthen you and give you the motivation you need, and the courage to grow stronger in doing His work for Him.

When your heart isn't satisfied, or your knees are trembling, kneel and talk to God.

Reminder: give thanks and be grateful for God's provisions every day!

Allow Jesus to live within you. Call on Him. Pray to Him. Praise Him. He is worthy, and so are you. Walk with Him.

Make your requests known to God and give Him praise with thanksgiving. Continue to persevere in praying.

If you don't pray currently, start small. Pray short sentence prayers. Pray, each new day adding a new sentence to your prayer (of thanks, or healing for someone, or for whatever). Do this for sixty days to get in the habit of praying. After sixty days, continue praying daily. Throughout your day - morning to bedtime, say a quick sentence prayer whenever something comes to your mind.

Allow God's strength, that is in you and in your hope, to help you to persevere today and always.

We must persevere, to continue, in a course of action even in the face of difficulty, with little to no prospect of success.

Persevere in your relationship with Jesus Christ because His clear purpose will stabilize your life. Persevering can bring about transformation.

Perseverance can create wonderful blessings and new beginnings.

LIFE

Whatever we do in life, most of it comes with companions of uncertainty and change. Sometimes, we can see one of these or both. Change always brings along uncertainty.

If uncertainty visits, change will arrive sooner or later. Clarity may or may not arrive to help, because it depends on how you deal with uncertainty and change.

Invite decision and decision's friends, clarity and understanding, to get solutions from uncertainty and change.

Never stop doing your best, especially for God and His works. Jesus lived a perfect life.

In everything—all circumstances and situations—turn to God in confidence for meaning, strength, courage, wisdom, and guidance of His power and of the Holy Spirit to see you through until the end.

The seeds of comfort may take root in the soil of adversity.

The trials and sufferings in our lives are our deserts. God strengthen us through trials and sufferings.

Are you complaining and grumbling instead of being thankful for the gifts God is providing you as He is strengthening you?

When we bear God's wonderful name, we must never do anything that would bring shame to His name.

Going forward requires sincere effort. If you are *un*able to take a big step, take baby steps forward. Taking those baby steps one at a time will create a huge impact and spectacular results in your life.

A godly life is all about Jesus, His death, His crucifixion, and His resurrection.

We are to live this life with a purpose to receive an eternal home forever. Life is all about what God thinks about us and the way we live, not what we think of God.

With a sharing heart, manage your life and what you have wisely. God can shift our thinking. Live your life under God's, our King's, authority.

Look beyond people's labels at the fruit they produce for Jesus. The fruit of our lives is what's important.

The older you get, the more you realize how dumb it is to be proud.

We are the person who determines where our life will take us after this earth is gone, whether that is heaven or hell, by how we live our daily lives here on earth.

THE WORD OF GOD

The Word of God is our guide for an amazing transformation.

There are absolutes in God's Word that describe what is necessary to have citizenship in heaven.

Who and what we are is very important to us as individuals and to one another. Our mission is to love one another as Christ loves us, to stay centered on the way the teacher Jesus taught, and to continue to build better lives on His firm foundation.

Expect things to be brought to light as you attend church or study God and His Word.

Appreciate the comfort and encouragement found in His Word, His presence, and His people.

God has revealed the future to us in His Word – in Daniel and Revelations.

Only when we live according to God's Word and ways will we begin to affect our world, our homes, and our society in greater ways. God can shift our thinking. Live your life under God's, our King's, authority.

Enroll in God's school. It's called the Bible. The Bible is the greatest educational opportunity. It teaches us how to raise children; how to be husbands or wives, how to show love and respond to our mates, children, family members, friends, and others. It teaches us how to live successfully in our careers and lives, how to act, and how to serve ourselves and others. It teaches us how to behave as employees and employers, how to honor our creator and our government, and how to live as people in all areas of our lives. Make time for God's Word: the greatest teacher in the world. We all are attending the "University of Life."

Are you succeeding or failing the assignments from the University of Life?

Continue to go to God's library, the Bible, which has sixty-six books in it. Some of the books are really letters written from Paul to churches.

The Bible speaks to special needs, concerns, longings, questions, and suffering. Find answers in God's Library.

The Bible will not let you down if you refer to it every day. It's the best guide for your life. Jesus is "the Bread of Life" (John 6:35 NIV).

"All Scripture is God-breathed and is useful for teaching, rebuking, correcting and training in righteousness, so that the servant of God may be thoroughly equipped for every good work" (2 Timothy 3:16-17 NIV).

Dig deep into God's Word. The Word of God has authority.

"All your words are true; all your righteous laws are eternal" (Psalm 119:160 NIV). God's Word contains power. All of God's words really are righteous, inspired, eternal, and truthful.

Our hearts and lives are to be centered on Our Heavenly Father's foundation. Each day strive to follow the written word of God and follow in Jesus' footsteps, striving to be the best servant you can be to Jesus Christ and to others.

Learn what is right and wrong by reading God's Word to avoid blurring the dividing line between right and wrong.

You're free to live the life of Jesus or not. It's your choice.

No one is responsible for your relationship with God but you. You are 100 percent responsible.

Pray for a greater awareness of God's Word, impressing it upon your heart, soul, mind, and conscience as you read and study His Word.

Reading and studying God's Word is not enough; we must obey it and apply it to our lives. Follow all the words of the law.

We can benefit from the wisdom and direction that come from knowing and living God's Word.

Do not rebuke the food of God's Word. Each teaching has a different taste.

The Word of God—the Bible—is still relevant today. God's nourishment keeps our hearts, souls, and minds healthy.

The scriptures will make you wise and successful if you take heed of them and live them.

Let's not ignore God's truth, which is His Word. Apply and follow His Word for a greater life on earth and the hereafter.

God giving us His truth in the Bible and His son Jesus are magnificent and awesome gifts.

If we follow the Bible's words, we will never perish.

Grow stronger in your faith by reading the word of God and find rest in God's arms for the rest of your life. "For no Word of God will ever fail" (Luke 1:37 NIV).

The Word of God brings liberty. Rejoice in Christ and in the gift of life in its abundance.

Reading and obeying the word of God is the recipe for many blessings and fewer worries.

"The Word of God is alive and active. Sharper than any double-edged sword, it penetrates ever to dividing soul and spirit, …, it judges the thoughts and attitudes of the heart" (Hebrews 4:12 NIV).

Lose your world's identity for Jesus Christ. Reading the Bible and praying prepare us for victory.

The Bible is a prescription for our hearts, minds, and souls. Jesus is the physician of all Christians.

In the Bible, God's Word basically says, "Do not give up. Do not become discouraged or dismayed for I know things you can't see. Keep believing."

The Bible contains guidelines for the good life. Live boldly with biblical optimism!

Live to do what's written in the best Book of Life, the Bible.

The Bible is the best guidebook to live by ever in history! It will not let you down if you follow it. Strive to do what is says.

Quit searching elsewhere for true purpose and meaning in life; go search the Bible, using the index to find the topic you desire. An alternative: search the Bible by asking Google for the topic you desire to find in the Bible.

We are led to deception when we read what we believe rather than believe what is written while reading God's word.

Reading, studying, and focusing on the scriptures and God are some of our assignments here on earth.

God and His Word are real and offer help for real life, and for all of life's circumstances! God does not force His will on anyone.

According to Pastor Talbot Davis, paying attention to what the Bible, or Jesus, didn't say points out how powerful Jesus and the Bible really are. So, notice what's not in the Holy Bible and notice what Jesus didn't say or do.

The Bible tells us that being a Christian is a great way to die, and following the Bible is the best way to live.

Search God's Word for answers, for guidance in everything, and allow God's Word to provide the answers you need for your life's problems.

If you are worried, facing challenges or concerns, dealing with grief, separation, or other challenges, find the topic in the Bible and read how to deal with the issues.

Proverbs in the Bible is full of wisdom and a wonderful guide to becoming successful, if you follow its teaching. There are thirty-one chapters in Proverbs. Read one chapter each day. Every month for twelve months reread the chapters in Proverbs. If you follow this advice, it can make you successful. For the months that have only thirty days, read two chapters on the first, or last, day of the month to complete the reading of Proverbs every month in the year.

Do not skip your Bible meals. Feed and nurture your heart and soul with God's Word and His love meals daily.

STRENGTH FROM GOD

God is our strength. God is our shield. We are nothing without Him. He gives strength to the weary and increases the power of the weak.

You and I can do all things through Jesus who has given us strength and stamina.

The Almighty Father has promised to strengthen us through every challenge and be with us through every hardship.

God is committed to caring for us, watching over us, and giving us strength when we are within His will. He cares for us every day, all year long, always.

Amid our afflictions, there is hope in God. Hang on to hope. God can give you hope during your loss or crisis. The Lord will renew the strength of those who hope in Him.

"The Lord is the strength of His people, a fortress of salvation for His anointed one" (Psalm 28:8 NIV). "The Lord gives strength to His people; the Lord blesses His people with peace" (Psalm 29:11 NIV).

"God is our refuge and strength, an ever-present help in trouble" (Psalm 46:1 NIV).

THE TRUTH

Have love, truth, and peace. Love the truth. Hate the *un*truth.

Grow readiness with godly courage, and always tell the truth.

Ask Google to find out what the Bible says about *truth* and about *lying* or *lies*. Or use the Bible index to find scriptures on truth, lying, or lies.

Learn and know the truth. Put God's words in your ears, mind, heart, and soul. Always be gentle and tell the truth. Things work out better when you do.

Always tell the truth, exercise justice, and live peacefully. Speak the truth with kindness regardless of what people want to hear, or don't speak at all.

Don't keep being *un*yielding or *un*willing to learn God's truth. God is true and good!

Let your life be an illustration of God's truth. Allow the Holy Spirit to guide you into all truth. Seek the truth in childlike faith.

Learn from children and animals. Children are so trusting. Children are humbly open to receiving.

Telling the truth will set you free (see John 8:32). Learn how freeing it is when you tell the truth even when it is difficult to be honest.

Open your eyes to the truth. "It is the Lord's purpose that prevails" (Proverbs 19:21 NIV).

Wisdom and truth are important in work, in marriages, in relationships of all kinds, and in all things, including conversations. Speak the truth always with kindness.

We need to seek God's wisdom and knowledge through His Word to establish His truth instead of allowing our own experiences to interpret the word of God.

Our words are to be the truth; otherwise, they are meaningless.

Our actions must back up our words, our commitment, and our promises.

Truth never changes. Telling the truth is always best. Telling the truth protects you and me from greater problems and hurts.

God's Kingdom will be managed by the truth; nothing but the truth is allowed in God's Kingdom. There will be no sin, no evil, and no wickedness in heaven's realms.

"The Lord is good and His love endures forever; His faithfulness continues through all generations" (Psalm 100:5 NIV).

God requires truth, goodness, justice, and righteousness, from all people—from you and me, and from all nations. When you and I resist the world, God renews us with the truths.

A truth which we need to validate in our experiences every day of our lives is that we were made by God our Father for His enjoyment.

Be truthful, be persistent, and stay on the righteous road while maintaining your integrity! The highway of truth is the way to travel and live.

Use God's truth as your weapon always. The nature of God is truth. And those who deal in truth are His delight.

All truth is embodied in Jesus. Be on the side of truth and listen to Jesus.

"Truth is like honey to those who have tasted lies" (unknown).

Time exposes many lies and falsehoods. Make it your quest to get God's truth into your character. "And the truth will set you free" (John 8:32 NIV).

SUGGESTIONS FOR ONESELF

Adopt this as a motto: I am loving, respectful, mindful, and encouraging of others.

Care about what God thinks! The choices you make in life become your breathing life.

Think about all the things you take for granted that are given to you each day, regardless of who the giver is or how you receive it. If you benefited from something (gifts of any sort), count it and heighten your awareness. Examples include light, darkness, heat, breeze, breath, sight, vehicle, pens, desk, bed, work, stove, home, food, people, an item,... Write them down—don't stop—and keep thinking and writing about the many ways you are blessed with gifts each day from God and others.

Show your gratitude for the gifts you receive daily in some way. Are many of the gifts the same? Yes, but don't take them for granted.

We lose our usefulness to God when we exalt ourselves in our own eyes. We need to change and become humble.

Don't be a critical person. Be sensitive to people while reflecting goodness and honesty to them.

Rejoice in your daily blessings. Represent Jesus and the joy of heaven.

SERVING OTHERS

Making others your priority is more important than what you yourself want; it will assist you in strengthening your abilities and help build your confidence as you become successful.

Listening and doing what is best for the others involved helps one to be more successful.

Strongly encourage others. Compliment people. Look out for "one another; have the same mindset as Jesus" (Philippians 2:5 NIV).

Concentrate on loving others and obeying God. Become less selfish.

We don't fully know how to embrace opportunities that are there for us because we see obstacles instead of opportunities. We fail to make better choices, allowing the obstacles to block our sight. Therefore, the obstacles stop us cold on our way to greater lives, greater marriages, greater relationships with others, and with life itself. Learn that obstacles can hide the opportunities that there; so look beyond the obstacles for what can be.

Let your spirit light shine along with your joy and your love.

Gently help others to see the dividing line between what's right and what's wrong, between what is sin and what is not sin.

Jesus desires mercy. Display love and mercy to others and be loving and merciful to all people.

Show mercy always. Exercise God's discipline and be discerning, not negative. Do not tear anyone down.

Help others when you are worried or feeling down and out. It leaves less time for self-absorption in what's worrying you. You will be blessing someone else and yourself. It will uplift you and the other person.

Insignificant people can have a great impact and make great contributions to society, to others, to family life, to churches, to communities, and so on.

Minister to the needs of others. We must remove all barriors to serve God fully.

We are to serve people, not use people. Look for ways to help others. Do not be above doing any job. Be a servant of God, a humble servant, and an unselfish servant.

Invest in God today and help others each day. Show love and kindness daily.

Let the fruits of your lips be honesty, thankfulness, acknowledgment, encouragement, forgiveness, and truth spoken with kindness.

Let the fruit of your lips be uplifting while speaking kind, loving words to others, and be thankful while confessing, acknowledging, and glorifying God our Lord.

I once heard or read that the poorest of the *poor may be the ones who live without Jesus and His love.* Many people are not accepting of the "Holy, Holy, Holy, Lord God Almighty, which was, and is, and is to come" (Revelation 4:8b).

Do everything in your power to learn and know the gospel of the kingdom, then share it with others.

Be a person using your tools: fingers, hands, feet, eyes... God provided you these tools for you to help others as well as yourself. Our tools are useful in helping ourselves and others get the work done more quickly than if we did not have them. God has greatly blessed us in magnificent ways.

God expects us to live out our faith; this means responding to those in need, being kind and loving to all people, giving forgiveness, being encouraging, being compassion, and giving assist to others when you see a need, ... always being Christ like – as a servant to all people.

Empathy is experiencing and feeling the burden of a person's heart that's dealing with agony or hardship.

OBEDIENCE

Obedience—being a faithful servant—is the test of faith. Respond to God in obedience by loving and assisting others.

Do not ignore God's warnings of obedience. Remember your maker: God our Father. He demands we prioritize obedience.

Obedience to God is possible and everyone can access holiness if they so desire by walking on the path of righteousness and by living and obeying God's Word.

God defines our destinies according to our obedience, our faithfulness, and our servanthood to Him through prayer and His Word.

If you obey and carefully follow all of God's commands, He will give you many blessings (more than He already does), and He will be with you to lead you.

Disobedience is the root of many people's problems, and the cause of misery.

Tithing, without obedience and love for God, amounts to nothing more than a ritual.

We will be judged by our unproductive lives. We must be active in our obedience to God and obey His teachings.

We must apply God's standards to our lives to help us grow in obedience to please our Lord God. Obedience is the pathway to eternity and heaven.

We must be obedient while continually confessing our daily sins, keeping God's commandments, following in Jesus' footsteps, and making Him the most important thing in our lives. We must keep Moses' and God's laws if we want to live with Jesus for an eternity.

Practice being obedient. Read His Word, learn His lessons, study His desires, and know His promises. Get to know Him and experience His goodness.

Our part is to yield to Him and be obedient as His vessels. We are to fully cooperate with God and follow His directions.

Know and keep God's requirements. He is our Holy Heavenly Father. Be wholehearted in your obedience to God. The prize is worth it.

True greatness comes about as we're serving, loving, and having compassion for others, being trustworthy, and by serving God through being obedient to His Word.

Nothing is more important than being obedient to God. God does not accept excuses. God wants your commitment and your obedience. Be determined to be a person who is committed and obedient to God.

God is delighted when we repent, and when we are obedient. Let the Lord be your light. Be a follower of God.

It is the fear of the Lord, and the punishment of living in an unquenchable, burning sulfur fire for eternity, that gives us the determination to be obedient to God our Lord. Imagine yourself burning and never dying in a fire much hotter than any fire you have ever known forevermore.

Always, live by God's standards. Faithfully be obedient to God's teachings and follow Jesus.

Live obedient to God's laws and commands so you will be invited to live in the beautiful and glorious city of Heaven, God's kingdom.

Let God's reward be your driving force, goal, and motivator for you to live an obedient life for Him so you can enjoy pure joy, peace, and love in His Kingdom, and enjoy the most beautiful place that is beyond your wildest dreams for an eternity.

PEACE

Jesus Christ is our peace. God gives us His holy spirit, love, peace, and joy when we accept Him.

Disobeying God's spiritual laws brings disarray and turmoil. Cooperation, fulfillment, love, and peace are the results if we obey God's spiritual laws.

Live with love, peace, gentleness, and compassion in your heart and soul.

God can give you peace in your heart during any crisis.

God can bring us healing when we are hurting or sick, peace when we are troubled, and strength when we are weak. Trust God.

When we're in the grip of God's peace, we touch the spirit fully. God's peace is like God Himself: perfect and infinite.

Have your ever experience the Holy Spirit's peace? It's indescribable and miraculous!

God's purpose is to remove sin completely, and to restore peace in the world.

Rest your mind in peace with God. Let Him protect you and keep you in His joyful peace.

Experience peace with God. Stand up and plead God's case.

No one else can walk your (or my) Emmaus Road. Open your eyes and ears to the fact that Jesus is among us, or beside us if you and I are believers. We cannot have true happiness and peace away from God.

The Bible is a book of wisdom that will lead you to peace, joy, and happiness. The Word of God is essential for a greater peace in life.

Concentrate on the requirements of God: fearing God, obeying His ways, serving Him with all your mind, heart, and soul, loving Him, and observing His commands so you can find peace.

HEAVEN / ETERNAL LIFE / GOD'S KINGDOM

Missing out on eternal life with Jesus Christ will be the worst of circumstances.

Deepen your love and longing for the life of heaven. In heaven, there will be no chaos, problems, sickness, tears, crying, pain, sorrow, or wars. There will be only peace, love, goodness, kindness, joy, singing, rejoicing, and worshipping God.

There is an eternal purpose as we live in faith. Each one of us must do his/her part to have access to heaven.

Think about the things of heaven, not the things of earth. (Colossians 3:2 NIV)

Have confidence in a new earth and new heavens; currently, there are three heavens according to the Bible. (see Deuteronomy 10:14, 2 Corinthians 12:2, 1 Kings 8:27, and Matthew 24:29)

Let your life be driven by eternity. Live to please God so you can be free of the fiery pit.

Value the eternal benefits that come from being a child of God and worshipping God. Allow eternal life to drive you.

God will be forever powerful on earth and in the heavens for all eternity.

Where will your future living quarters be: Heaven or Hell?

Eternity is placed within you at birth. This is the reason you have longings. When you believe in Jesus Christ, give your heart to Him, and become a follower of Him, this desire for eternity will be fulfilled. The Holy Spirit that you receive within fulfills your longings; therefore, no more longings will exist if you stay connected to Jesus Christ.

We each need to realize we are building lives today, not just here on earth but for eternity. We are building lives where we will live with Jesus for eternity, or lives (away from Jesus Christ) of death in a never-quenched fire, with worms that never die, for eternity. We all will live forevermore in hell or in heaven.

Reference eternity by asking questions like: "Have I ever thought about living an eternal life after death?" "Am I ready for eternity?" "What eternity home am I currently pursuing with my actions and speech?" "Am I currently living for the perfect eternal life of heaven with Jesus Christ?"

How we build our lives will determine how we fare when eternity comes. Nothing impure will enter heaven!

Understanding God's plans and knowing how to live as His servants are vital for eternal life with Jesus.

We must believe in and follow Jesus and live God's Word to have an eternal life with Jesus Christ.

Everyone who hears, reads, and lives God's Word and puts His Word into practice is wise and is building a firm foundation for a new home in heaven. That person will have God's solid foundation from which to weather the storms of life.

Being a disciple is an investment in your new eternal home and it yields great rewards.

Be careful not to lose the heavenly home by your lack of faith or by having the wrong attitude and motives. Thank God that He provided us a way to heaven and a new heavenly home.

Let go of the familiar so you can step into the heavenly realm.

God has given us access to heaven through His son Jesus.

Free grace allows us access to our Father in heaven.

God's suffering servant, His son Jesus Christ, lived and died as the payment for our sins. Jesus was restored to life (resurrected) as the hope of the world, giving new life to the followers of Jesus Christ, so all followers could have eternal life forever.

We need to consider the central component of the larger whole: believing in Jesus, Jesus being born as a baby, crucified on the cross, resurrected, ascended into heaven, and will be returning one day… and the believers that have repented of all their sins, living in obedience, being faithful, loving all people, having compassion, and living by imitating Jesus Christ and have been baptized will be welcomed into heaven. These are the necessary components of a pass for us to get through heaven's gate, so we can spend eternity with Jesus.

Our inheritance, as true Christians, is eternal life with Jesus Christ.

On the other side of this world—in heaven—there will be no more pain or sickness, no more tears, and no more sorrow. What a glorious time that will be! There will be only pure hearts and words in heaven.

We must do two things if we want eternal life. We must obey the first and second commandments: "Love the Lord your God with all your heart, and with all you soul, and with all your mind. This is the first and great commandment. And the second is like it: 'Love your neighbor as yourself.' All the Law and the Prophets hang on these two commandments" (Matthew 22:37–40 NIV). Know that we are to live by all the commandments and commands that are spoken from the many prophets and from God that in the Bible.

If we ignore God's gifts, the inspired Word, or Jesus' teaching, we will live an eternity in an unquenchable fire – hell.

God made the first move: He gave us life, grace, and love. He gave us His only Son, and He is offering us eternal life. Will you accept His gift of eternal life?

Start preparing yourself for a better eternal life, for the life you want after this earthly life is over. So that you may live, choose life in Jesus Christ!

His kingdom has no place for selfishness. Learn to put God's desires and others' needs before your wants.

Live with your eyes, heart, mind, and soul on God and the things of the Kingdom, not on the things on earth or the difficulties in and of this world.

If we want the glory of the kingdom (eternal life), we must be united with the crucified Christ, our Lord Jesus. The mercy of God is what rescues us when we repent.

We are vulnerable to teachings that only speak of what it is we want to hear. We must really know God's words, to know what is and isn't acceptable to enter into the kingdom of God. Otherwise, we may fail to meet the requirements that are needed to enter through the pearly gates of heaven.

"Seek first His kingdom and His righteousness, and all these things will be given to you as well" (Matthew 6:33 NIV).

MISCELLANEOUS

Who we are in representing and in believing Jesus Christ, as our savior, and repentant are more important than anything else.

Discipline helps to keep children going in the right direction.

What seems harmless can soon spin out of control and wreak great destruction.

Self-discipline helps keep teens and adults centered in the right direction.

I heard someone say, "It's badness itself that's bad."

Lack of guilt isn't a barometer of whether we are doing what is right.

To prevent failure, learn from your failures. Failures assure future mistakes and possibly other failures, especially if you do not learn from each of your mistakes. Let your past failures and mistakes point you to a greater future.

Saying *no* to God leads to disaster. Saying *yes* to God brings new understanding of God and His purpose. The confidence you place in God will not be in vain.

Contamination rubs off on others, but Holiness does not. It's too bad it's not the other way around: holiness rubbing off on others.

If you stay focused on God and make smart choices, you will never regret focusing on Him. You will have more success and confidence as you grow stronger in doing what's right.

Humility comes from wisdom.

I heard a minister refer to a person who said that integrity is keeping your word even if the circumstances change after the promise was made.

When we look at the dark side of life, we take ourselves into the darkness. It's a better life to stay in God's light.

When people surrender their wills over to God, it is wonderful what miracles God can (or will) do with their willingness.

Moment-by-moment and day-to-day life is not always clear. We can't explain what we don't understand.

Every problem can teach you something if you examine the problem.

There is a job for you and me to do in this beautiful place called Earth.

Pastor Talbot Davis said one Sunday, "You can admire Jesus all the way to hell or follow him all the way to heaven."

The best person you can have in your life is Jesus.

Someone once said, "If you enjoy and love Superman, you should really love, enjoy, and praise the greatest superman who ever lived: Jesus. He is miraculous and the most powerful of all supermen."

Your future is within your grasp. Let Jesus be your leader all the way into His kingdom.

Jesus intended His church to be a place where we "Carry each other's burdens, and in this way you will fulfill the law of Christ" (Galatians 6:2 NIV). You and I are to carry one another's burdens to display God's love so others can witness His love is alive in us.

If you and I make no effort to affect the world around us for better, we are too much like the world and are worthless. We need to be witnessing, uplifting, and affecting other lives in positive ways.

To know Jesus is to know His life and life that's abundant and eternal. Living for Jesus, many difficulties will vanish if you allow God to hold your hand daily through your endeavors. "Whoever seeks good finds favor" (Proverbs 11:27 NIV).

I heard a minister say that Jesus can't be a little great or a little significant. He is *significant!*

False prophets and Satan's helpers will come in friendly packages, wolves wearing sheepskin. Be alert. They will seem harmless but are deceptive. (see Matthew 7:15 NIV)

The Ten Commandments and commands are not just idle words for you; they are for your life on earth and are meant to give you eternal life. Command your children to obey carefully all the words of this law. (see Deuteronomy 32:46–47 NIV and Exodus 20 NIV)

Stand firm in honoring the Ten Commandments that the Lord our Savior gave to Moses and the teachings of the prophets including commands of Jesus. The Ten Commandments expose our sin. We are to listen, obey, and live the teachings including the commands throughout God's Word daily. If you stick with Jesus, He certainly will stick with you.

Majestic works prompt majestic responses.

Accept Him today and trust Him. Jesus Christ came and died to give us every blessing if we trust Him.

Each of us is recognized by our fruits and behaviors: our speech, minds, souls, deeds, and actions express who we are and bears the fruits accordingly to how we are in all of these areas.

"Do not be afraid. God has come to test you, so that the *fear* of God will be with you to keep you from sinning" (Exodus 20:20 NIV).

The only way to improve the churches is by attending and improving ourselves.

You can't imagine all that God has in store for you when you truly trust Him. God uses us as His vessels.

God will give you victory if you keep God in your life where He belongs.

You cannot teach a person who doesn't want to listen.

An idol is anything that is reverenced more than God.

Pastor Talbot Davis at Good Shepherd Church in Charlotte, North Carolina, has said, "Do not let what you have accomplished, up until now, be the greatest thing you ever do."

We do not start out bad, but choices trap us, and influences grab us. Resist any unhealthy traps and influences. If necessary, remove yourself from these types of situations.

Excuses are disguised through rationalizations by the person who is doing the rationalizing. They are false explanations. Get rid of excuses.

Effective people are forward thinkers for the good.

Our attitudes define us because they come from our hearts and tell people who we truly are. Why? Because our attitudes create our actions, our actions create our reactions, and our reactions create our results.

Giving mercy and showing grace knock down obstacles.

The key to victory is trusting God even before you know what it is He wants you to do.

Confession releases God's loving grace and mercy.

If we live for Christ, our spirits will glow, showing others *what* Christ is about.

Sabbath is a memory method so that we can remember to worship God totally with our hearts, minds, souls and strength.

The Sabbath, a day of rest, is a gift from our loving God. Do no work on the Sabbath. Keep the Sabbath holy.

"It is lawful to do good (for others) on the Sabbath" (Matthew 12:12 NIV).

FAITH / FAITHFUL / FAITHFULNESS

Faith is believing while acting upon God's word. Faith and courage go together and are partners.

Faith without action is dead faith. Lack of faith blinds us to the truth and robs us of hope.

Wait patiently in faith and be confident in God. He is in control. Be a faithful fan of God's assignments for life.

Hold fast to your *faith* in God and know that God Is sovereign!

God will deliver the faithful ones who follow Him, and the reward will be great! Make sure you are found faithful in God's eyes.

Faithfulness to God has a rich reward, especially in the eternal life to come.

We do everything in faith: driving; sleeping; sitting; walking; going into buildings; eating the food presented to us in restaurants, by our families, and by others as we faithfully trust the food hasn't been poisoned and that the food has been prepared correctly; trusting we won't get sick; trusting we will get well; trusting that we'll arrive at our destination safely; ... We trust in God: in the light of the sun, in the darkness of the night, and in the rain that He provides to the earth for our livelihood; in God's continual gift of breath, in having oxygen to breathe; and in the flexibility that gives us movement. We trust also in many other things.

We have faith and we take our daily provisions for granted when we ought to show our gratitude daily and be thankful for God's daily mercy, grace, and provisions every day.

Give God credit for what He does in your life. Praise God when He answers your prayers, or when you receive a blessing, and be faithful to Him always.

Always be prayerful, loving, joyful, and faithful.

Do not compromise your faith in God. Be wise and secure your future in Christ. Believe and obey the one true God. Have courage and put your faith in God.

Live faithfully according to God's desires. The faithful will not be forgotten. Faithfulness is the chief requirement of God. Let faith have you!

God will deliver His faithful children. They will live forever—for all eternity.

If you are not ready, get ready. It simply takes faith in God, and a willingness to act on that faith, to live a Christian life.

Faith is about planning and moving forward with God as your life's director. Always hold firmly to faith. Be dressed in faith for the King's triumphant return.

Our God reigns! He will rescue His own. Our faithfulness is required for us to be included in God's faithful souls.

Be found in right living. The body is dead without the Spirit as faith is dead without deeds. (see James 2:26 NIV)

Gratefulness happens when we faithfully *follow* God and obey Him and His commands.

Lack of faith blinds us to the truth and robs us of hope. Our faith, or lack of faith, affects us, and others, in the things we do, or don't do.

Our faith need not be hindered by our struggles and sufferings. There is an eternal purpose as we live in faith. Faith is believing while acting upon God's word.

First comes faith, second comes belief, energy, and efforts, then our expectations produce our results. To attain the best, we must expect the best and do our best.

FEAR

When the Bible says, "fear God", fear of God is not negative, but a positive attitude of reverence (great respect). Reverence Him like you would your own earthly father or mother, knowing that if you do something wrong, you will be disciplined. God disciplines his followers.

Fear (reverence) of God keeps us from displeasing Him. Otherwise, we may fall into Satan's traps. Say no to fear, complacency, and comfort, and move forward by faith in God's love and power. Fear of God gives us strength to stay steadfast in our obedience to Him.

Know that true fear is not from God. Therefore, eliminate the deadly condition of fear through God by praising Him.

TAKE ACTION…

The power of action is much greater than the power of words! Action is like TNT: much more powerful than words.

Allow God to reshape you into a valuable vessel. Trust in the Lord and center your life on God and His work.

Let us strive to be God's helping hands by

- helping to comfort the hurting or sad;
- helping those who experience tragedies;
- helping the sick in their needs;
- helping those who are needy (physically, spiritually, or mentally);
- helping those dealing with death, illness, or loneliness;
- helping those who are lost and searching and wanting to know what's right;
- helping those feeling overwhelmed and hungry, such as the poor and needy;
- praying for the persecuted, the sick, the elders, and the homeless;
- praying for the lost and dying world as God's ambassadors;
- praying for those experiencing tragedy;

- praying for our government, the president, senators, majors, all divisions of military, and everyone in any leadership position throughout the United States;
- praying for *all* people who are leaders in any segments in government, and *all* business leaders of each state in the United States;
- praying for *all* judges, clergymen, doctors, practitioners, and nurses, policemen, and detectives;
- praying for *all our schools, the children,* teachers, *churches, and religious organizations.*

I once heard someone say, "Do something today that will matter for tomorrow and for the future today."

"Ascribe to the Lord the glory due His name; worship the Lord in the splendor of His holiness" (Psalm 29:2 NIV).

Let knowing God and godly action be your greatest priorities. Be a light for Christ. Overcome this world.

Honor all people! Show people the love of Jesus even through their worst behaviors.

Point people in the right direction by using love.

Give hope to others, encourage them, and support them in their times of need. We all have had times of need. Show them God's love through the love He gave you.

Distinguish between the holy and the common. Love and be concerned for all people, the saved and the lost, the good and the wicked.

When you rise in the morning, think of what a precious privilege it is to be alive: to breathe, to think, to smell, to see, to enjoy, to love, to move, to walk, to hear, to have choices, ... Give God the gratitude He deserves because daily He provides and gives you and me everything we have.

Live up to God's ideas of fairness and His rules. And do what really counts in God's eyes while repairing your life by applying the laws and principles of God's Word.

Purge away *un*necessary priorities and diversions – media, x-box, idols, etc.

Demonstrate God's Holiness as you look forward to your future home in His kingdom.

Look for windows of opportunity in your situations to share Christ in some way.

Don't limit God's work in your life by underestimating Him.

Take the focus off your problems to focus on what is good and right in your life and give thanks to God. Recognize the good that comes out of bitter experiences.

Make sure you are willing to take your own advice as you teach or lead others. (I need to do better on this item as well.)

Make it your life's goal to always do those things that will please the Lord Jesus Christ. Make God the main thing in your life and follow His commands.

Live life according to how God is directing you to live if you are interested in eternal life in heaven. Take your eyes off the world and turn them on God.

Have continuity with God. Honor God and keep your step in the right direction. Watch God work in your life and find security in His sovereignty.

Decide on your commitment before situations appear. Develop staying power and serve God wherever He puts you.

Trust God to protect you in ways you may not be able to see. Find a way to live by God's standards.

Never compromise God's laws. Remind yourself that God is watching your every move. Trust God with your past, present, and future.

Do what is just and right! Be respectful to God and to all people. Look beyond yourself. Let your empathy and compassion shine.

Let go of the obstacles and embrace those opportunities! Embrace the privileges that God has given you!

Strive to live differently and better each day in this world. Start by making a minor change for the good and continue until it becomes a habit. Continue to repeat this step.

Never be happy about others' misfortunes. Act compassionately to stop injustice. Take a vow to be of service to and for God by being His servant.
Apply God's laws to yourself instead of thinking about what others need to be doing or are doing. Do away with self-centeredness and have compassion for others.

Hand over yourself and your cares to the Lord: your soul, body, mind, thoughts, prayers, hopes, health, work, job, life, and death. Also hand over your family, parents, spouse, siblings, neighbors, friends, country, and love to God for all people always.

Instead of having *demands* or *definite* desires, have *preferences instead* so you can have an easier life.

Put on your new nature, be renewed in your Creator, and become more like Him.

Begin doing the right thing. Just start, even if you begin with baby steps.

Let your actions be right and pleasing to the Spirit of God so you will reap eternal life.

Allow your burdens and troubles to cause you to cling to God. Cling tightly to Him.

Seek God so that you may live forever with Jesus in His heavenly home. Admit you cannot save yourself; your only hope is in Jesus Christ our Lord. Lean on God always.

In God's sight, you are worthy of His love. Give God His rightful place in your life. Make sure nothing comes before Him.

Never leave God out of your plans or life. He will do so much more than you can on your own.

Give God His rightful place in your life. Make sure nothing comes before Him.

Let God dress you in His goodness. Do what you can where you are and leave the results up to God.

Remain pure, one day at a time. Strengthen your faith in God! Always obeying His commands.

Sow righteousness to reap mercy and loving kindness. Stop neglecting God's spiritual priorities and fulfill your spiritual duties. Be sure you do your part; God will do His part and keep His word. You can count on this!

Put God's words into actions. Be a person of love, of prayer, of Bible study, and of worship.

Listen to God's Word and do what He says. Do what your Heavenly Father desires for you.

Diligently "fully obey the Lord your God and carefully follow all his commands" (Deuteronomy 28:1 NIV).

"This is what the Lord Almighty said: 'Administer true justice; show mercy and compassion to one another" (Zechariah 7:9 NIV).

Stop your foolish deeds so you can stop them from multiplying; then, increase your wise deeds so they can be multiplied swiftly. Allow your life to become a channel of blessing instead of a comedy of errors.

Refuse to give into bitterness and hatred. Give your heart, your bitterness, and your hatred over to God.

Allow God to give you a new heart. Surrender to Him. Let go of your troubles and pain. Place them into God's hands.

Place your anguish that you have into His hands. Our richest moments are of divine service. Move into the fullness of God's will.

Sense God's desires and dreams for yourself. They are birthed through prayer.

Live a disciplined life mentally, spiritually, physically, and emotionally. Put your faith into action.

Live with deeper faith and sharper focus on God, His character, His promises, His accomplishments, His gifts, and His blessings He provides.

Ditch pessimism. Turn your mental anguish over to God and put on a "can-do" positive mindset full of energy.

Move past the pain of the past. Get help if necessary. Declutter your mind, life, and routine. Live more simply with God in your life. Give Jesus His rightful place as king of your life.

Challenge yourself. Put God first and give to God first.

Allow God to guard you against a fruitless and hypocritical life. Surrender to the authority of the Lord.

Change your ways. You and I must be ready. Do His work of His kingdom now so you will be prepared for His return.

Turn your ordinary work into an opportunity to influence others for His Kingdom.

Share Christ Jesus with people. Share in His victory. Be a part of a successful story for God.

Serve the Lord with gladness. Everything belongs to God. Be patient. Keep striving to live into Jesus' righteousness.

Strive to work with integrity and strive to live with loving and caring behaviors. Be faithful to our Father as Jesus lived.

Trust in Him and be secure. Our King is returning, and He will reign forevermore.

Forget the past and look forward to what lies ahead. Find purpose in your life to go forward into your tomorrows.

Use leverage to grow. Your life is far from finished.

Go forward with the plan God has for you; as a believer, press on to eternal life.

Look to Jesus for your spiritual guidance in prayers and keep your faith in Him. Pray scripture verses. For example: "Teach me your way, Lord, that I may rely on your faithfulness; give me an undivided heart, that I may fear your name" (Psalm 86:11 NIV).

Give the same time you now spend on social media, news, and the like, and spend that time with God. You and your heart, mind, and soul will grow and change, and become more beautiful.

Fix your eyes not on what is seen for what is seen is temporary, but on what is unseen for it is eternal, for Jesus will prepare us a place forevermore. (see 2 Corinthians 4:18 NIV)

Keep the presence of God in the center of your thinking. Put God first and give God your best every day. Leave behind those things that keep you from following God's Word.

When you think of doing something good, take the necessary action(s) to make it happen. *Hold* onto what is good and *reject* evil. Learn the lessons that history has already taught.

Stop being an enemy to yourself. Each person is his or her worst enemy. With a glimmer of hope, take courage and carry on.

Observe the practice of praising, tithing (giving at least one-tenth of your earnings to God) and thanking God for His wonderful blessings. Refusing to tithe is like robbing God.

Allow God to guide you while you're on an earthly journey toward a heavenly home.

Put your mind where you want your body to go and on what you want your voice and hands to accomplish.

Prepare for new ways to serve, new ways to uplift people, and new ways to live.

Walk in victory by putting time into a relationship with the Lord.

Learn to be content with whatever the circumstance is. Continually draw upon God's name and power.

Never avoid doing right because of what others think or might think. Shine God's promises and power on your problems.

Persist in pursuing God, and know that living for God takes faith, focus, and follow-through. You will be rewarded.

Be eternally sure of your final destination. Move forward to your greatest eternal potential.

Continue to pray for more love, wisdom, knowledge, and understanding.

Always look upon your words to see if they match your actions, and to see if your words and actions produce good fruit.

Seek and desire God's approval, not people's approval. Remain receptive to God's guidance.

Align your ways of living in the spiritual image of Jesus.

Reach out to Christ in faith and reach out to others in the faith that God guides you with.

Get your life right! Live by looking toward the future, toward Eternal Life. We are recognized by the fruit we bear.

Cultivate hope through your thoughts and actions. Continue to move and go forth in Christ and in life.

Continue to carry the shield of faith to extinguish all the ways of the evil one and the wickedness of this world.

Put on the full armor of God, so that when the day of evil comes, you may be able to stand your ground, … Stand firm then, with the belt of truth buckled around your waist, with the breastplate of righteousness in place, and with your feet fitted with the readiness that comes from the gospel of peace. In addition to all this, take up the shield of faith, with which you can extinguish all the flaming arrows of the evil one. Take up the helmet of salvation and the sword of the Spirit, which is the word of God. And pray in the Spirit on all occasions with all kinds of prayers and requests. With this in mind, be alert and always keep on praying for the Lord's people. (see Ephesians 6:13–18 NIV) Always carry these tools with you wherever you go.

Allow God to be your security guard and let our Lord God watch over you. Keep God in the center of your life by putting your faith in God and be willing to follow Him.

Create a new mind filled with gratefulness and thanksgiving to God and to others, especially to your wife or husband and children. Show them your love and gratitude for what they do.

Work on removing your selfishness and replacing it with love and compassion. Live within the established boundaries of God's word.

Stabilize your life by purposefully walking with God with all your strength, heart, mind, and soul.

Live with a biblical perspective and be strong and courageous every day! Don't let your strong will cause you to disobey God's wisdom and commands.

Get ready to be spiritually lifted on a higher level by the Holy Spirit while you are on this earth while following God's Word.

Continually examine yourself through God's eyes and requirements. If you don't know God, read about Him in the Holy Bible. The Bible is the "number one" best seller book in the whole world and has always been the best seller of all books. It's not fiction. It's about real people, God, His Power, His followers, life, death, sinners, sin, marriage, laws, battles, work, promises, love… and so much more. I suggest you start with the New Testament and Proverbs. Proverbs is the book about how to and how not to live life, and how to be successful. The Bible is a library of 66 books.

Enjoy a fresh renewing of yourself to God and His ways as you continue to guard your heart and mind with God's help.

Have eyes to see with the heart. Have ears to hear with the heart. Have actions that speak from the heart of God's love and have lips that speak the truth.

Enjoy being in the presence of the Lord instead of rejoicing in sin; rejoice in love, kindness, and goodness.

Trust that the King of Kings is returning some day! Get to know the Lord our King by reading and respecting the Living Bible.

Put into place a way to stay strong in the Lord God – reading and mediating on the word of God each day. I suggest the same time morning, or/and night, daily.

Remove all that's too weak, too tired, or down and out from yourself, and all negativity, which will make you a quitter.

Give up all your negative thinking and negative talking in your mind and in your vocabulary. Replace your stinky thinking (or thoughts) by training yourself to look at what's right, what's good, and what's working.

Each morning say, "The Lord is my strength, through Him I am able to do whatever is needed today."

Pour out your concerns to God. Tell God your deepest needs and concerns, earnestly and humbly.

Live single-mindedly for Jesus so you can enjoy the earth He has given to you and the heavenly mansions He is building for you.

Have the courage to stand up for a God perspective, not a worldly perspective. Win by being a champion for Jesus so you can win the award of heaven and more.

Ask God to help you to get honest with yourself, and with others. Open your heart. Be receptive. Line up in the acknowledgment of God. Declare God as your Lord of your life!

Honor God with your body. Give up any rebellion. Align yourself with God.

Strive to live peacefully with all people in godliness and holiness – loving, caring, and helping all people.

Take and give all your small problems to God before they turn into big problems. Call on God, the perfector of your faith, to accompany you in whatever you do and wherever you go.

Never loosen or relax your courage. Hang on to your courage and do not be faint-hearted. Jesus is your restorer.

Ask the Holy Spirit to lead you to repentance and restoration to God, to cleanse your thoughts, speech, attitudes, and motives at their sources.

Lay hold of what Jesus Christ has offered you and everyone else. Always act nobly and do what is right.

Ask God to re-pattern your heart and mind with a greater design, which can take you to your eternal home.

Ask Jesus to sustain you through your crisis and know that He will. Rest in God's arms and ask Him to give you strength and peace through the pain that seems endless.

Have the spirit and grace of self-control through believing and following Jesus Christ.

Keep seeking God and His heavenly spiritual realm. Make your strongest desire living close to God and His Word. Liberate yourself through God.

Do your spiritual exercises for greater godliness. Put your mind on things of Heaven, on blessings, on the good that is taking place, and on the Word of God.

"Trust in the Lord with all your heart, and lean not on your own understanding; in all your ways submit to Him, and He will make your paths straight" (Proverbs 3:5–6 NIV).

Pray to God asking Him to replace your anxiety, to fill you with His power, to give you His protection through any crisis and problems, and to fill you up with His love, mercy, and grace.

BE... BECOME...

Be bold and diligent.

Be useful to other people.

Be driven by great love, compassion, and mercy.

Be encouraged by the words of hope and have hope in the perfect kingdom of God.

Be determined to follow God wherever He leads you.

Be a champion by leading others on the right path of helping people who have been less fortunate than you.

Be prepared for the dark deceptions by learning what the book of God says.

Be thankful in hearing God's wisdom and wise people's corrections. It means God and wise people love you. God wants you in His kingdom.

Be careful from whom you take authoritative advice.

Be a thankful person. You have so much to be thankful for.

Be confident that God will guard and watch over you if you are observing His commands and are righteous in the sight of God.

Be "confident of this: I will see the goodness of the Lord in the land of the living. Wait for the Lord; be strong and take heart and wait for the Lord" (Psalm 27:13–14 NIV).

Be on guard to keep your priorities straight. Put first things first by putting God first.

"Be alert and of sober mind. Your enemy the devil prowls around like a roaring lion looking for someone to devour. Resist him, standing firmly in the faith" (1 Peter 5:8–9 NIV).

Be concerned about bringing and winning people to Christ.

Be responsible for your choices every day. Be a blessing to the world. Let God lead you.

Be determined to obey God, doing whatever He asks of you and going wherever He leads you.

Be a missionary, wherever you are, for God.

Be honest in your dealings.

Be just and right in giving or doing what you say you will give or do. Be defined by our risen King, the King of Kings.

Be careful in how you build your life and home life. Allow Jesus Christ to be your strong foundation.

Be determined to serve God and let your first allegiance be to God.

Become locked into giving of yourself positively; love, help, and do the right things for yourself and others. Teach and serve others out of love.

Become God's conduit for those around you.

Become the master of your thoughts. Stop letting your thoughts be the master of you. Take control of your thoughts so you can have a better life and a less stressful life. Feed your mind uplifting thoughts.

Become God's obedient child, a servant, and a follower of His. God hates pretense and hypocrisy.

Become a forward-thinking and a focused friend to others to encourage them forward.

Become willing to please Jesus Christ. What would pleasing Him look like to you?

SPIRITUAL WORLD

In the spiritual world, there are absolutes and benefits to being a believer and faithful child of God.

Spirits that are evil and good are all around us. Which spirit are you following or serving?

"This is how you can recognize the Spirit of God: Every spirit that acknowledges that Jesus Christ has come in the flesh is from God, 3 but every spirit that does not acknowledge Jesus is not from God. This is the spirit of the antichrist, which you have heard is coming and even now is already in the world" (1 John 4:2-3 NIV).

Your soul is spirit. It wants to connect to its source, which is God the Father, and to abide in the great source, God.

Holy living comes about when we are empowered by God's Holy Spirit. We need God's cleansing.

We are cared for by God's Holy Spirit. God's spirit is with us and within us if we are a follower of Jesus Christ. Be sensitive to the Holy Spirit and allow Him to lead you always.

One day, if we are followers of Jesus Christ, we will be like His spiritual image.

The Holy Spirit is our trustworthy pilot taking us to heaven. Through God's Spirit, lasting value is accomplished.

Allow the Holy Spirit to move you. Listen to your heart and follow His instructions.

The flesh and spirit conflict with each other, so you are not to do whatever you want. "Walk by the Spirit, and you will not gratify the desires of the flesh. The flesh desires what is contrary to the Spirit, and the spirit is contrary to the flesh. They are in conflict" (Galatians 5:16-17 NIV).

The Holy Spirit is the stimulus of our souls, hearts, minds, and strength; "If you are led by the Spirit, you are not under the law" (Galatians 5:18 NIV).

It is evil (Satan), or the goodness (Holy Spirit) who control or doesn't control you and your actions. So, blame only yourself for responding to the wrong spirit if things go badly. Say to Satan: Get behind me, Satan! Jesus said to Peter, "Get behind me, Satan! You are stumbling block to me" (Matthew 16:23 NIV).

If you are a Christian, the Holy Spirit is the one trying to guide you, whether you listen, or not, it's your responsibility. Listen to the prompting of the Holy Spirit and allow Him to be your guide.

The meaning of Luke 3:4 (NIV) "Prepare the way for the Lord, make straight paths for Him" is saying we are to turn our lives away from sin, and be obedient to God. Therefore, our lives are to reflect the decision that we have turned toward God within our minds, hearts, souls, and bodies so God's Holy Spirit will guide us and empower us to live into righteousness.

The Holy Spirit of God gives us peace and freedom from fear. We will succeed only through God's Spirit.

God's Holy Spirit and power are here with us. With God's help, we all can grow more sensitive to the Holy Spirit's presence and toward others.

"May the God of hope fill you with all joy and peace as you trust in him, so that you may overflow with hope by the power of the Holy Spirit" (Romans 15:13 NIV).

By nature, we are objects of wrath, but anyone can be made alive through Christ and His Holy Spirit. Take the steps to have a transformative life in Christ.

DEMONIC POWERS - SATAN

I once heard someone say: Believing that demons and demonic powers aren't real is a dangerous place to be.

Know that Satan and his demons are very real. Even the demons knew Jesus. (see Mark 1:34 NIV, Mark 1:23–24, Mark 3:11, and Mark 5:12).

Untruths, unfaithfulness, forsaken vows, and hateful words inflict wounds and shatter relationships. Know that these things are Satan at work within you and me.

Jesus came among us to give you and me freedom from sin and Satan's control.

The devil is not afraid of the people who have a Bible that stays in a drawer or closet, or those who do *not* read it. Absorb the treasures that are found in the Bible that are given to us all to find.

If you refuse to follow Jesus Christ, you have chosen to be on Satan's team.

Jesus has complete power over Satan and Satan's forces. Know in the very end, Jesus Christ is returning and will overcome Satan and all evil.

Wrong desires coming from Satan's spirit will result in wrong actions and turn people away from God.

Satan seeks to destroy those who trust God and put their faith in Jesus Christ. Stay alert. Satan is an enemy. Always tell Satan to *get behind thee.* (It's Okay to stomp your foot when you tell Satan to get behind you.)

"Put on the full armor of God, so that you can take your stand against the devil's schemes" (Ephesians 6:11 NIV).

Satan is deceitful. He tricks people into sin - into doing wrong. And Satan uses friendly and charming people that are wolves disguising themselves as lambs.

"Satan himself masquerades himself as an angel of light" (2 Corinthians 11:14 NIV).

The devil's schemes are like quicksand: you can be drawn into the quick schemes, and before you realize it, you are deep within the quicksand. You're caught in Satan's schemes quicker if you don't recognize *all* the signs of sin. Most all stumbling blocks are from Satan. Remember to tell Satan, "Get Thee behind me." (Read Matthew 10:16, Ezekiel 22:26-31, Colossians 2:8, Romans 16:17-19, 2 Timothy 4:3-4, 2 Corinthians 11:14-15.)

We have two choices: one is living as a believer, a follower of Jesus Christ; the second is living intentionally as a sinner for Satan and for oneself. We should, and need to, know where we stand.

Insensitivity and negativity destroy relationships and marriages and are acts of disobedience to God. These downfalls are caused by demonic spirit influences.

It's *im*possible to be neutral about good and evil. Evil is choosing to be separated from God.

Satan is a hindrance; God is a great blessing and a friend.

God would never tempt us to do harm or evil. All things wrong and evil come from Satan.

Although it may be easier to be an influencer for Satan, be an influencer for the Lord, *not* for Satan. It doesn't require accountability, or much strength, or thought to be an influencer for Satan. Strengthen your accountability to God.

Just know you will *not* be blessed by the devil. No one will ever be blessed by Satan. Rebuke Satan by keeping God's requirements.

All negative talk is from the spirit of Satan and is not uplifting. Do not allow sin (Satan's spirit) to bring judgment and condemnation upon you.

Do *not* let Satan continue to have your mind, heart, and soul destroying you and others.

It's better to offend Satan than it is to offend God. Satan is offended when God's people pray.

We communicate our actions or lack of actions, our words or lack of speech, and our responses or lack of responses, through our body language, whether we are children of God or not. Do you behave with love that glorifies God? That is, are you a witness for God's good, or for Satan's evil?

My desire is that you and others will be encouraged to make a greater effort to live *less* in serving the spirit of Satan and *more* in serving the spirit of God. We should all have a godly passion to reduce negativity, gossiping, complaining, and accusations in order to help defeat the current worldly passion for condemning, accusing, and putting people down without having all of the full facts.

DO NOT...

Do not put off the decision to follow Jesus and be His disciple. Nothing is to be placed above total commitment to living for God. Base everything, all your decisions in life, on Jesus' Word.

Do not be blinded and oblivious to your need for God.

Do not postpone your preparations for eternal life with God our Lord.

Do not just read God's rules then close your eyes and heart to God's intent. Understand the reason He made and gave His commands. He did so because He loves us and wants us living with Him in His kingdom always.

Do not be ruled by what is convenient and neglect your responsibilities.

Do not stay locked into negativity. Focus on Jesus' road ahead, not on the one that you are stuck on or have traveled previously – unless you are on the narrow road to heaven.

Do not let corrupt communication proceed out of your mouth.

Do not worry about today, or the tomorrows. Trust God totally!

Do not become a stumbling block to anyone or hinder any good deeds.

Do not let anxiety, indifference, hate, dislike, or anything else hold you back. Push forward for a better life.

Do not let social pressure, or fear, dictate what you do. Do what is right! Do what Jesus would do. Be true to God. He will reward you.

Do not let money, or your desire for prestige, keep you tied to a job or position you should leave.

Do not let anyone or anything come between you obeying God.

Do not treat God like a light switch, turning Him on and off. Always rely on God.

Do not ignore your spiritual life. Ignoring God will lead you to ruin.

Do not take lightly the warnings in God's Word.

Do not lie. Each person is accountable to God for his or her words, actions, and works.

Do not try to bend God's will to fit your will.

Do not reject the warnings of judgment.

Do not violate God's laws.

Do not steal, practice immorality or idolatry, behave wickedly, swear falsely, work on the Sabbath, dishonor your father and mother, kill, covet, or lie.

Do not let the schemes of Satan draw you into his demonic activities in your life.

Do not reject what is good. Allow God to change your behavior. God knows all of our evil thoughts and deeds.

Do not allow your mind's thoughts to turn into action which will take you to Hades—the forever never-quenching burning fire. Change your thoughts and actions in the direction of God's purity for a life forevermore in heaven.

Do not allow your own smoldering, festering, and enticing desires drag you away from a beautiful life with Jesus—an eternal life in a most gorgeous place than you can imagine.

Do not allow anyone else to separate you and your love from God's presence.

Do not let worldly desires, busyness, or pride to choke the gospel out of your heart.

Do not blame God for your struggles and troubles.

Do not allow worry and fear to destroy your confidence or destroy the abundant life God has given you to live.

Do not blame others. You have three fingers pointing toward you when you point to another person. Blame yourself for making the wrong choices, for not taking the proper actions, for not doing what was required of you, or for not managing your time. Do not be a creator of more problems.

STRUGGLES / PAIN

When you face problems, ask yourself if these problems would have been smaller if you had had a different attitude and behavior, or if you had displayed more caring and loving actions to another person.

Struggles mature and complete us because they shape and mold us. They make you and me more resilient.

Give God all your worries and fears. He can handle them. Fear and worry only bring more fear and worry. Continue to fix your eyes and heart upon God's love and power and His Word instead of on unnecessary fears and worries.

Lay aside your worries, fears, and heaviness by praying and placing them in God's hands, and by trusting Him and His promises.

Refrain from judging! Many times, we are so sure we have all the facts when we really don't. We have all been guilty of jumping to conclusions and spreading rumors by gossiping, condemning, using accusations, and putting down people without having all the facts of the whole storyline. Why? Because our memories aren't always right in all the facts. Remember, there may be little to no truth in what someone said, or what someone thought he or she saw, or what someone thought he or she remembered. Always give people the benefit of the doubt. Behave as Jesus would in all types of situations: with love and grace.

Allow Romans 8:28 to alter any burden, discouragement, and all emotional pain, to reduce strongholds of painful emotions of grief, and to impose confidence in your heart. "We know that in all things God works together for the good of those who love Him, who have been called according to His purpose" (Romans 8:28 NIV).

Our greatest problem is human's sin and disobedience to God. Oneself is the problem for one's results.

Ninety percent of our difficulties take place because we are not doing God's will.

Seek God in times of difficulty, discomfort, and struggles.

When we are brokenhearted, our feelings can devastate us. God is still with us. He gives you and me the strength to get through the pain.

Suffering develops strong character and deep wisdom.

Joy comes after weeping.

No situation can control us if we fully forgive, allowing God's faith and power within. He gives us endurance.

KNOW THAT…

Know that *your input* determines *your output*.

Know that you win when no one is watching. And with God in your life guiding you, you are better than you believe you are, more capable than you realize, and stronger than you think you are.

Know that Christ Jesus' kingdom will replace and surpass the world.

Know that God needs to be our greatest priority.

Know that God is watching you. He sees and knows everything you think, say, or do—whatever that may be, and whenever and wherever you say or do it.

Know that when you accept Jesus in your life as your Lord, you are making a priority statement. Jesus gets to set the boundaries, guidelines, limitations, values, and applications for your life.

Know that His Father, God, gave you and me the scriptures as our guide to read so we can know what is expected of us and how to live for Him and how to live a successful life.

Just know that you and I are powerless without Jesus Christ. We must repent and reform our lives if we want heaven as our homes. We must build solid foundations with Jesus Christ.

Know that for much of what goes wrong for us, we are to blame—not others, not God, but we are to blame for not doing better than we did. Ask for forgiveness and repent; then, forgive yourself and any other people that was involved.

Know that the Word of God says by the blood of Jesus we are redeemed out of the hand of the devil if we have repented of our sins. All our sins are forgiven. We're cleansed from all sin if we continuously repent of any new sin. We are justified and made righteous, just as if we had never sinned.

Know that "whoever is not with me is against me, and whoever does not gather with me scatters" (Matthew 12:30 NIV).

Know that a "good man brings good things out of the good stored up in him, and an evil man brings evil things out of evil stored up in him" (Matthew 12:35 NIV).

Know that if you have given your life to God by confessing within your heart, if you have affirmed with your mouth that you believe in Jesus and His resurrection, if you have been baptized, if you sincerely have repented of your sins to Jesus Christ, and if you are living the Word of God, Satan has no power over you because you are a child of God through the blood of Jesus Christ.

Know that our gracious soul desires more of God.

Know that the more you trust God, the easier it gets. It's the same as when you keep doing something, such as exercising; the more you do it, the easier it becomes.

Know that the more we depend on God and His Word, the stronger we will grow spiritually.

Know that even when you don't know, know that He knows all things, and that you can trust God. We are never out of God's sight.

Know that the most important thing is to live with God as your Lord, Savior, and Master.

Know that the safest place to be is in the center of God's Will. It's the most satisfying, and the most rewarding place to be.

Know that we are living in the wilderness with God on our way to the promised land of heaven.

Know that Jesus Christ is the best model you have for you and your children, for your marriage, and for your life.

Know that God is important to our lives. He is central to life. God must be our first and foremost priority! Include Christ Jesus in everything you do.

Know that God wants loyalty. Commit to God with deep and sincere loyalty. Then back it up with your actions.

Know that *everything* is meaning*less without God*!

Know that nothing can break God's promise to protect His people.

Know that your life is to be lived as a living sacrifice to God. (see Romans 12:1 NIV)

Know that Jesus loves everyone but hates their evil and *all* wrong doings.

Know that God wants to make us a blessing and light to others. Let your light shine upon others. Remember the song "This Little Light of Mine" and let your light shine.

Know that God will most likely not change us until we acknowledge Him as our Lord.

Know that God holds us responsible for our actions and choices. Be abundantly forgiving.

Know that we have God's instructions for how to live, how to act, and how to be!

Know that God wants changed lives. He wants His people to be loving, compassionate, just, merciful, fair, and humble. Be upright with integrity.

Know that the most important part of life and of the church is God's presence.

Know that God is more than adequate to carry you and me through all of life's difficulties and challenges.

Know that *all* people were created in the living image of God.

Know that no matter how low you are in this world, or what you have done, there's no limit to what God can do in your life if He is the carpenter (center) of your life.

Know that God wants to resurrect you and me from the inside out.

Know that God wants us to be sincere and faithful in all areas of our lives.

Know that God deserves our very best—honesty, respect, faithfulness, prayers, and love—and so do other people.

Know that God wants us to have a can-do attitude daily, and to have endurance and perseverance to do His will.

Know that God can help us and will help us if we follow Him. Leave your past behind and commit your future to Him.

Know that the Lord is concerned about you. This should give you a purpose: to live for Jesus, knowing you can have a life forever in an eternal home with Jesus.

Know that what we give God, and do for God, reflects our true attitude towards God.

Know that happiness in the Lord gives us joyful strength.

Know that when we neglect or abuse others, including believers, that we are serving Satan and we are neglecting and abusing God.

Know that God wants to do more within us, and when we walk with Him, we will discover the good in us deepen each day.

Know that our abilities and gifts are given to us by God. He supplies our every need.

Know that trust and thankfulness to God will take you to great places, in work and in life.

DECISION / INDECISION

God has prearranged and made ready a good life for you. However, that offer of a good life depends on the choices that you make. Make the decision to follow God's Word.

Always seek God's wisdom, especially when the decision affects others, then follow through regardless of the difficulty.

It is your decision to obey or *not*. Just know your decision is a life-or-death matter; hopefully, it's a sentence for an eternity in heaven. Choose life with Jesus in His Kingdom!

Don't let your eternity in Heaven be lost because of poor decisions or indecision.

Whatever we decide will have eternal consequences! Ground *all your* decisions in prayer.

Everything you do comes from a decision you made. Make better decisions for a greater life.

Indecision causes more failures than poor decisions.

Everything we do is a decision, including giving to God through tithing or *not* tithing; loving one another or *not* loving each other; showing kindness or *not* showing kindness; and bearing good fruit or *not* bearing good fruit while we are here on Earth.

Christ Jesus our shepherd will never force us to follow Him. We make the choice to follow or *not* to follow Him. Make the right decision and follow Him. Remember, you are the one who must make the decision for yourself. Neither God nor anyone else can make that choice for you.

WE MUST… WE ARE… WE NEED…

We must know God's Word, what it says and what it means.

We must apply God's Word to our daily lives if we want to live with Jesus forevermore.

We must resolve to obey God and to stand against the onslaught of temptation.

We must be prepared to sacrifice ourselves by suffering for God to support others. Do you show great love to others?

We must purge any evil from within us or among us.

We are responsible for any wrath upon ourselves.

We are all leaders in some capacity, good or bad.

We are here to make God look good, not make ourselves to look good.

We are to do *good* works, as God prepared us to do.

We are to submit to God inside and outside—in our hearts and with our bodies—obeying the Ten Commandments and all other commands.

We are saved when we repent of our sins and continue to live into His righteousness; and if we believe that Jesus Christ was born of a virgin, that He died on the cross, that He was resurrected, that He ascended to heaven, and that one day He will return.

We are to stop seeing people as we humans do and start seeing people as Jesus does: as individuals to love, help, and support - always with kindness.

We are to be doers for Jesus Christ. Begin the journey of intimacy with Jesus Christ.

We need to seek God to discover what He wants us personally to do.

We all need new souls and minds, and news of greater love and kindness.

We all need to admit we cannot save ourselves. Only Christ Jesus can save us!

We need to be in compliance with God, following His Word. God gives understanding and insight.

We all need to look to Jesus Christ our Lord, who has given us everything that we need so we can make a major impact on this earth for the better.

We all need to live rightly and justly by wisdom and consideration, and exercise prudence and patience.

We all need to be concerned about our motives and attitudes as much as we are about our actions. We will be held accountable for our attitudes, motives, and behaviors.

We all need to approach God sincerely and graciously, caring for His Holiness and our reverence for Him. We should prepare our hearts and minds before Him and for Him.

We need to praise God, worship Him, trust Him fully, and glorify Him by giving Him the glory that He so greatly deserves.

We all need to listen, watch, and act according to God's Truth while showing love and compassion in our actions.

We need to please the commanding officer, Jesus Christ. And we need to train ourselves to be godly.

We need *hope daily*. Life is all about daily hope and believing.

We need to read God's Word and seek His Holy Spirit, which are our life's GPS system. God and His Word are perfect and powerful. Seek and use them in everything every day.

QUESTIONS TO PONDER

What will it take for God to get your attention?

What characteristics are you taking on?

Where are you going to spend eternity according to your actions and beliefs today? Will you be living with Jesus in heaven, or will you be where Satan will be, in the burning fire that's never quenched in Hades?

What have you done for the kingdom of God?

What are you feeding your heart and soul?

What are you substituting for your god? Your mobile phone? An app on your computer or phone? Certain internet links? An X-Box? TV? Media?

What are you giving most of your time to? Media on your cell phone, TV, X-Box, your computer, or the Word of God - the Bible?

Are you giving God any time, or sufficient time in praying, in being thankful, in showing gratitude, in worshiping, or in praising Him daily?

What or whom do you love?

Is God speaking to you? Ask God, *Is there anything I need to change, or stop doing?* Then listen and follow as He directs you. Listen and obey His (soft) still small voice and the nudges you experience. They will serve you well if you listen and follow them. (His still small voice is so soft it seems surreal.)

Why should you and I be color blind when you and I can have pure light and be blessed?

Do you need to change your present behaviors, or actions, to follow Jesus Christ?

Where is your interest? Is it in yourself, in success, in others, in doing evil, or in God's work in helping others and doing good with a thankful and joyful heart?

Are you insensitive, lazy, insincere, or arrogant? Or are you sensitive, active, sincere, loving, and caring?

Would God be pleased with you? With your behavior? With your responses?

How are you reflecting Jesus to your family, friends, co-workers, and others?

Would you have fewer problems if you showed more love to your mate, family, others, and to God?

Would you have fewer problems if you gave your best at work and at home?

Examine yourself: your soul, your heart, your mind, your motives, your actions, and your thoughts. Our attitudes display who we are and affects others and our daily lives. Are you affecting others positively or negatively?

Does your attitude, thoughts, and actions reflect Jesus Christ or Satan?

Hate evil and love God. What is your character reflecting: good behavior or bad behavior?

Pastor Talbot Davis at Good Shepherd Church in Charlotte, North Carolina, asked, "What if your greatest achievement isn't something you do, but is someone you raised? Or, what if your greatest achievement is someone else you saved to be a witness as a servant of God?"

Are you being sinful? Or being righteous?

Are you willing to search for the treasures of God?

Is your name written in the Lamb's Book of Life?

What would happen if you took the role of Jesus' servant?

Do you deserve the same criticism as you place upon someone else?

Are you magnifying others' faults while excusing your own faults?

Why torment yourself by *not* forgiving? Forgiving others is for your own mental freedom and happiness. If you haven't tried it, try it with someone you haven't forgiven and see how freeing it is.

What perspective are you going to choose, God's or the worldly perspective? Choose the purest.

How do you give to Jesus Christ's kingdom?

Have you given to Jesus or His Kingdom today?

GOD IS:

- Love
- Loving
- Merciful
- Righteous
- Peaceful
- Joyful
- Pure
- Admirable
- Noble
- Truthful
- Praiseworthy
- Perfect
- Powerful
- Great
- The Almighty
- Victorious
- The Kingdom
- Glorious
- A prayer-answerer
- A miracle-worker
- A physician
- Luminous
- Trustworthy
- Holy, very holy
- The Holy Spirit
- Our Lord
- Our Father
- Omnipotent
- Omniscient
- Omnipresent
- Omnificent
- Benevolent
- Immense
- Pure spirit
- Alive
- Unlimited
- Unique
- Christ Jesus
- The Redeemer
- A healer
- Exalted
- Magnificent
- And much more

TO DISCOVER GOD'S PRESENCE AND PURPOSE

- Pray,
- Diminish distractions,
- Focus on God's Word and eternity,
- Believe in Jesus and His Resurrection,
- Have faith,
- Love all people,
- Invest, and leave an eternal legacy,
- Take risks - move out of your comfort zone or safety net,
- Make sure all your dreams and plans fit into God's plan and His Word,
- Pursue your dreams that's within God's plan,
- Finish—do not quit,
- Rejoice in God's goodness and celebrate,
- Give up all known sin: adultery, lying, cheating, false witnessing, stealing, coveting, idols: excessive TV, media, X-Box, Gaming, … mobile phone, and internet if it is causing you to sin.

WAYS TO STOP GOSSIPING

- Change the subject.
- Walk away or leave.
- Ask the other person to change the subject.
- Turn down invitations to pick others apart.
- Let the person know you're trying to break the negative gossip habit.
- Don't whisper in the presence of others.
- A whisper separates close friends.
- Defend the person because gossip separates the best of friends.

SCRIPTURE

"Wisdom Bestows Well-Being"
Proverbs 3:1–35 NIV

> My son, do not forget my teaching, but keep my commands in your heart, for they will prolong your life many years and bring you peace and prosperity.
>
> Let love and faithfulness never leave you; bind them around your neck, write them on the tablet of your heart. Then you will win favor and a good name in the sight of God and man.
>
> Trust in the Lord with all your heart and lean not on your own understanding; in all your ways submit to him, and he will make your paths straight.
>
> Do not be wise in your own eyes; fear the Lord and shun evil. This will bring health to your body and nourishment to your bones.
>
> Honor the Lord with your wealth, with the firstfruits of all your crops; then your barns

will be filled to overflowing, and your vats will brim over with new wine.

My son, do *not* despise the Lord's discipline, and do *not* resent his rebuke, because the Lord disciplines those he loves, as a father the son he delights in.

Blessed are those who find wisdom, those who gain understanding, for she is more profitable than silver and yields better returns than gold. She is more precious than rubies; nothing you desire can compare with her. Long life is in her right hand; in her left hand are riches and honor. Her ways are pleasant ways, and all her paths are peace. She is a tree of life to those who take hold of her; those who hold her fast will be blessed.

By wisdom the Lord laid the earth's foundations, by understanding he set the heavens in place; by his knowledge the watery depths were divided, and the clouds let drop the dew.

My son, do not let wisdom and understanding out of your sight, preserve sound judgment and discretion; they will be life for you, an ornament to grace your neck. Then you will go on your way in safety, and your foot will not stumble." When you lie down, you will not be afraid; when you lie down, your sleep will be sweet. Have no fear of sudden disaster or of the ruin that overtakes the wicked, for the

Lord will be at your side and will keep your foot from being snared.

Do not withhold good from those to whom it is due, when it is in your power to act. Do not say to your neighbor, "Come back tomorrow and I'll give it to you"—when you already have it with you. Do not plot harm against your neighbor, who lives trustfully near you. Do not accuse anyone for no reason—when they have done you no harm.

Do not envy the violent or choose any of their ways.

For the Lord detests the perverse but takes the upright into his confidence. The Lord's curse is on the house of the wicked, but he blesses the home of the righteous. He mocks proud mockers but shows favor to the humble and oppressed. The wise inherit honor, but fools get only shame."

1 Timothy 3:16–17 NIV

All scripture is God-breathed and is useful for teaching, rebuking, correcting, and training in righteousness, so that the servant of God may be thoroughly equipped for every good work.

ROMANS 8:18 NIV

> I consider that our present sufferings are not worth comparing with the glory that will be revealed in us.

Ecclesiastes 12:13 NIV

> Now all has been heard; here is the conclusion of the matter: Fear (Reverence) God and keep his commandments for this is the duty of all mankind.

Exodus 15:2 NIV

> "The Lord is my strength and my defense; He has become my salvation. He is my God, and I will praise Him, and I will exalt Him."

Psalm 139:13–14 NIV

> The maker and author of our life is God.
> The psalmist states, "For you created my inmost being; you knit me together in my mother's womb. I praise you because I am fearfully and wonderfully made; your works are wonderful, I know that full well"

BIBLIOGRAPHY

Tharp, Devin. "God and the Broken-Hearted." Good Shepherd Church, February 14, 2020.

Printed in the United States
by Baker & Taylor Publisher Services